Exploring the Evidence:
Initiatives in the First College Year

Wendy G. Troxel and Marc Cutright, Editors

National Resource Center for The First-Year Experience® & Students in Transition ◆ University of South Carolina, 2008

Cite as:

Troxel, W. G., & Cutright, M. (Eds.). (2008). Exploring the evidence: Initiatives in the first college year (Monograph No. 49). Columbia, SC: University of South Carolina, National Resource Center for The First-Year Experience and Students in Transition.

Sample chapter citation:

McDowell, L. L., & Phillips, C. Y. (2008). Millersville University. In W. G. Troxel & M. Cutright (Eds.), Exploring the evidence: Initiatives in the first college year (Monograph No. 49, pp. 9-14). Columbia, SC: University of South Carolina, National Resource Center for The First-Year Experience and Students in Transition.

ISBN 978-1-889-27160-6

The First-Year Experience® is a service mark of the University of South Carolina. A license may be granted upon written request to use the term "The First-Year Experience." This license is not transferable without written approval of the University of South Carolina.

Special thanks to Dr. Barbara F. Tobolowsky, Associate Director, for project management and copyediting; to Dottie Weigel and Jonathan Romm, Graduate Assistants, for copyediting; to Tracy L. Skipper, Editorial Projects Coordinator, and Trish Willingham, Editor, for proofing; and to Ann C. Jennings, Graphic Artist, for design and layout.

Additional copies of this monograph may be obtained from the National Resource Center for The First-Year Experience and Students in Transition, University of South Carolina, 1728 College Street, Columbia, SC 29208. Telephone (803) 777-6229. Fax (803) 777-4699.

Library of Congress Cataloging-in-Publication Data

Exploring the evidence : initiatives in the first college year / Wendy G. Troxel and Marc Cutright, editors.
    p. cm. -- (The first-year experience monograph series ; no. 49)
 Includes bibliographical references and indexes.
 ISBN 978-1-889271-60-6 (alk. paper)
 1. College student development programs--United States--Case studies. 2. College freshmen--United States--Case studies. I. Troxel, Wendy G. II. Cutright, Marc, 1952- III. National Resource Center for the First-Year Experience & Students in Transition (University of South Carolina)
 LB2343.4.E94 2008
 378.1'98--dc22

2007049831

Contents

Section 7
Problem-Based Learning (Discipline-based)

Section 8
Student-Faculty Interaction

Preface

As students enter colleges and universities with various levels of preparation and prior experience, educators are not only concerned about retaining them but also about providing them the kinds of experiences that will enrich, and even transform, the way they view education. This monograph, drawn from presentations at the 25th Annual Conference on The First-Year Experience in February 2006, provides an in-depth look at how 22 colleges and universities, both two- and four-year, are using a variety of initiatives to improve student retention rates and make the first year a more meaningful and engaging educational experience. Many of these initiatives are also embedded in larger institutional cultures and value systems so that they meet institutional learning objectives while also responding to student needs.

If you have read other volumes entitled *Exploring the Evidence* from the National Resource Center, you will note that this volume is quite different. Rather than focusing exclusively on first-year seminar courses, the evidence reviewed herein results from the implementation of a variety of first-year initiatives that range from those that are course-based, such as first-year seminars or first-year mathematics courses, to those that are far more comprehensive. It will not surprise you that learning communities are the focus of several of the case studies. And you will want to be sure to read the entry about the comprehensive Michigan Community Scholars Program, a total living-learning environment that produces significant positive outcomes including a nearly 100% first-to-second year retention rate. Some of the programs feature new approaches to advising and intervening with students who have excessive class absences early in the term. Others describe the integration of service activities into the first year through learning communities, first-year seminar courses, and other activities. Increasing students' knowledge about and connection to surrounding cities is an important component of several of the initiatives, and successful in-class strategies, such as the use of peer leaders, problem-based learning, and course-related activities, are also described in detail.

You will find that this monograph goes far beyond simple descriptions of program components in that each entry also includes substantial attention to program objectives and how those objectives were evaluated. And I commend the authors for their candor as they occasionally acknowledge disappointments or the need for mid-stream changes because programs did not realize their desired outcomes. I am also pleased to note that retention was not the only outcome measured. Reported program results include increased student learning, positive changes in students' attitudes and behaviors, increased levels of meaningful interaction with faculty and other students, and improved academic skills.

This monograph is testimony to the substantive changes that are being made in first-year initiatives in this first decade of the 21st century. Attention to the first year is taking many forms beyond traditional pre-term orientation or first-year seminar courses. As the years go by, first-year educators are becoming more and more successful in imbedding innovation into the overall first-year curriculum and in reconfiguring basic institutional structures and processes to more effectively meet the learning needs of today's new students. Instead of being a year characterized by low expectations and low levels of engagement, the first year on many campuses is beginning to set the standard by which other years in the undergraduate experience are measured.

This monograph is yet another reminder to me that first-year educators constitute a viable and effective community of practice, one that is characterized by a readiness to share experiences and ideas with others. Whether you are reading this monograph in order to compare your institution's existing first-year efforts to others or seeking new ideas that work, you will find much to consider and emulate in these pages. And I hope that you will read "outside" your institutional sector. By and large, all of these first-year approaches are adaptable to two- or four-year, rural or urban, large or small, and public or private institutions.

I am confident that you will find this monograph a valuable addition to your library of first-year resources. The cases are well-written and concise. But they also include an optimal level of detail that makes them especially valuable to others who want to attempt the same strategies on their campus. The authors' honest recounting of "lessons learned" is an especially important feature. No one attempts to paint an artificial picture; rather, authors willingly share the rewarding, as well as the difficult, aspects of their work.

I applaud the monograph editors and the case study writers for their willingness to contribute to the growing body of research on first-year initiatives. I hope this volume will serve as a catalyst for you and for others to consider sharing your ideas and experiences for the benefit of all who care about the success of new students in higher education.

Betsy Barefoot
Co-Director and Senior Scholar for the Policy Center on the First Year of College
Brevard, NC
September 20, 2007

Foreword

Scholarly practitioners have been coming together annually for more than a quarter century to share best practices and lessons learned on a multitude of topics and initiatives related to the first year of college. The National Resource Center for The First-Year Experience and Students in Transition's Annual Conference on The First-Year Experience provides faculty and staff across multiple disciplines and institutions a showcase for successful program designs and strategies for student success, as well as the opportunity to share results of assessment activities conducted on first-year topics. It is this commitment to systematic assessment design, under the framework of solid education research, that prompted *Exploring the Evidence: Initiatives in the First College Year.*

As our collective call for better evidence of student learning and development grows within higher education and the public sector, it is clear that educators who work with first-year students must advance the agenda. In fact, an open discussion at the 25th Annual Conference about the future of research on the first college year revealed much agreement about the need to do more research but little agreement about appropriate designs and methodologies—with the quantitative vs. qualitative debate highlighting a prominent false dichotomy. The more relevant discussion focused on exploring those educational initiatives with strong assessment designs and implementation plans directly connected to the use of results. Research on the first year is complicated by the fact that most programs and services for first-year students are not housed in isolated departments or units but rather involve a much larger network of students, faculty, and staff within the institution.

Better evidence of learning is born out of a collaborative process of discovery that is based in systematic inquiry. So this monograph is part of a continual attempt to coordinate and further legitimize scholarly work on the first year of college under the framework of intentional programs and services. It is consistent, in fact, with the past 25 years of focus on the first year of college. The submissions that follow explore the design and assessment of curricular and cocurricular initiatives in a number of areas of focus, including

- Civic engagement and service-learning
- Early identification and intervention
- First-year advising
- Linked learning communities
- Organization and assessment of multi-layered programs
- First-year seminars design (i.e., planning and assessment)
- Problem-based learning
- Student-faculty interaction

Each area of focus is important to the educational experience and has its own set of intended outcomes, activities, and assessment methods, but it is also important to identify integration opportunities and monitor intentional strategies and results. In fact, first-year students are "touched" by virtually every part of campus, so collaboration across the institution is critical. And while each campus is unique and has its own special culture, there are also consistencies in how students tend to grow and benefit from the efforts of faculty and staff who help, so the initiatives that follow represent a wide range of programs, courses, and services that move us closer to tighter oversight of institutional efforts in the first year of college, with specific attention to collaboration and assessment.

Notable Examples

This volume incorporates essays that embody notable and quality indicators of the design, delivery, and evaluation of programs for the benefit of first-year students. In particular, we see multiple examples of these best practices:

Programs are not singular, isolated "silver bullets" but are integrated into a larger institutional philosophy and strategy. Individual programs can produce measurable and positive results, but their impact is substantially muted if they are not part of a more holistic approach to the first year of college. Essays here consistently demonstrate connection to a larger and more complex strategy of institutional action. No single program will address the challenges to success faced by all students, and issues of success and progress by students are socially and educationally complex and so should be our mutually reinforcing efforts to assist them.

There is a consistent presence of explicit, measurable, and a priori goals for programs. Too often, we see programs that excuse a paucity of evaluation by saying, "We haven't looked at our effectiveness yet; we're only two years into the effort." But resources, including our own energies, are scarce commodities. If we don't state clearly what we intend to accomplish (as often as possible) and how we'll measure it, we won't be able to identify the standards to evaluate what we're doing. Peter Drucker's "management by objectives" for business had and has as a primary virtue the ability to evaluate our efforts in real time. We should be able to do this, too. Our students have only one first-year expeience, and knowing what we might have done three or four years later is of little benefit to them.

There is a campus-wide approach to the establishment of objectives, program design, instructional and developmental strategies, and assessment. Student affairs offices are often on the cutting edge of first-year program development (such as orientation and transition activities), and academic departments have responsibility and expertise in the curriculum and the formal educational environment. A blending of strengths and perspectives from faculty, staff, and administrators not only results in better programs but also in better support for programs during their development.

Evaluation of programs is an ongoing commitment. Summative evaluations—the final, "how did we do?" type—are important, but so are formative evaluations—"how are we doing and how can we improve?" The best programs are marked by this continuous evaluation so that relatively minor but important adjustments can be made while the program is in progress. A certain kind of courage is required to undertake this critical evaluation of self and others, but once established as a habit and the benefits realized, formative evaluation has many champions.

Administration is on board. The importance of strong administrative support is perhaps most obvious when dealing with its absence: The commitment to programs lasts only as long as office incumbents, funding is soft, the assignment of quality personnel isn't a priority, and the promotion and reward system bypasses those with first-year and program commitment. Administrators can use their "bully pulpits" to build support from students, faculty, staff, administrators, and even alumni and trustees. Their involvement is also a benefit to administrators, who can show tangible first-year commitment to the institution's many constituencies.

Elements of Concern

We believe that a general and commendable trend over the past two decades is an increasing emphasis in first-year programming on both the articulation of specific goals and the incorporation of evaluation strategies into programs at early stages. These developments are compatible with the culture of evidence that is a foundational value in the academy and important to program support and continuation in our era of tight resources. Most importantly, good program evaluation heightens our confidence that we are making real differences for students.

But our examination of a multitude of conference presentations for potential inclusion in this volume suggests to us several areas of concern. As much as we laud current efforts and are proud to help draw attention to some best practices, we point to a few common concerns that can be instructional to program designers and implementers. Others have noted these concerns in different contexts, but we think it helpful to note them here. They include:

Very few data sources or a single source are used to evaluate programs. When we purport a range of beneficial outcomes for a program but depend heavily or exclusively on a single statistic or focus group to demonstrate effectiveness, it suggests that the evaluation plan is not well considered or was a tacked-on afterthought. Learning is complex and multi-dimensional. When possible, so should be our means of evaluation. There may be different ways to get to the same conclusion, but even that is helpful and makes our evidence base richer.

Retention is too often touted as the primary or exclusive outcome of an initiative. Retention is, without our charges and goals, relatively simple, if that's all we seek. We can, for example, just lower the bar of standards so that more can jump it. The trick is to pursue enhanced retention while also creating a challenging academic and social environment in which real intellectual and personal growth occur. While increased collaboration between academic and student affairs is a hallmark of our recent progress, if we allow the legitimate administrative concern of retention to conflict with the legitimate academic concern of challenge, we set this trend back. Both sets of goals should be part and parcel of our programs and their evaluation. A retention number without context is a small piece of a much larger puzzle.

Insufficient consideration is given to the "volunteer effect" in evaluation. Pilot programs and others are often populated by volunteer students, leaders, and instructors. The results of the program are then examined by comparing results, say GPAs, of the pilot group against the general student body. But common sense, let alone a rich research base, makes it reasonable to assume that the most interested and motivated students led by the most interested and motivated teachers are going to do better on average, regardless of the programmatic framework. This is not to say that such data are not important, but if they are the primary means of judgment, the differences should be substantial (not merely statistically significant), replicable, and on a fairly substantial scale of involvement.

The research base is sometimes scant or not apparent. It sometimes seems that we are not only in the success business, but the wheel reinvention business as well. The body of literature on other programs, their results, and their recommendations for adaptation is now so rich that to ignore it is simply poor practice. Knowing what has worked elsewhere—and what hasn't—gives us both a great head start on design and credibility in acquiring support for initiatives. Sometimes, we reject that approach because "we're really different" from any other college or university. Every environment is different from all others, but our challenge is to see what's common, or adaptable, and to benefit from that experience.

Summary

The authors of the case studies that follow are to be commended, then, not only for their comprehensive approach to student learning and development in the first college year, but also for their willingness to share "lessons learned." Real world replicability happens best when we model the most fundamental aspects of learning, that is, being challenged to move beyond the safety of what we already know and being willing to fail as well as succeed. We encourage you to review the initiatives with an eye toward those aspects that resonate with the educational issues you face on your campus and to continue to share your research in public arenas.

Wendy G. Troxel
Illinois State University

Marc Cutright
University of North Texas

Section 1
Civic Engagement and Service-Learning

Georgia State University

Institution Profile

Atlanta, GA
Public, Four-Year
Civic Engagement and
Service-Learning

Editors' Notes

A large, research university in the heart of Atlanta, Georgia State University offers students an important opportunity to expand the learning environment. Atlanta-Based Learning connects students' classroom experiences with the local community at multiple levels through a variety of lenses. The four anchor components (Learning about Atlanta Settings, Learning from Atlanta Systems, Learning with Atlanta Communities, and Learning by Atlanta Service-Learning) allow faculty and staff to incorporate a wide range of curricular and cocurricular activities while maintaining focused oversight for student engagement.

The Institution

Georgia State University, located in downtown Atlanta, is a public, four-year institution. It is the second largest university and the only urban research institution in Georgia. Predominately a commuter campus, Georgia State began offering residential options in 1996 after the Olympic Games. Athletes from around the globe lived in the Village, which was later transformed into housing for 2,000 students. With an additional 435 spaces at the Lofts, and 2,000 spaces at the University Commons opening in fall 2007, the university continues to see growth in traditional age first-year students.

In fall 2005, Georgia State University had 13,752 full-time undergraduates with 2,211 first-year students and an overall enrollment of 25,945 students. Georgia State, the most diverse institution in the state, enrolls students from every county in Georgia, every state in the nation, and more than 145 countries. Student demographics are 54% White, 28% African American, 11% Asian, 3% Hispanic, and 3% multiracial/other. In terms of gender, Georgia State is 60% female and 40% male. First-generation students, defined as students whose parents do not have a bachelor's degree, constitute about 11.5%. Undergraduates over the age of 25 comprise 22.4%.

Description of the Initiative

In August 2004, the Office of Undergraduate Studies launched Atlanta-Based Learning. The initiative promotes the university's strategic mission to increase involvement within the downtown community and increase student retention.

Atlanta-Based Learning promotes academic and civic engagement within the greater Atlanta community. As a metropolitan, research institution, Georgia State offers the opportunity for students to make connections between academic courses and the urban Atlanta environment by participating in the life of the city around them. While engaged in Campus Atlanta, students link their learning to its urban surroundings. Atlanta-Based Learning charges students to become active learners using Atlanta as a backdrop and encourages them to give back to the community. The program integrates service-learning opportunities and community engagement activities throughout the academic curriculum and across disciplines. Undergraduate and graduate students can participate individually or as a class in Atlanta-Based Learning along a continuum of engagement encompassing four components: (a) Learning about Atlanta Settings, (b) Learning from Atlanta Systems, (c) Learning with Atlanta Communities, and (d) Learning by Atlanta Service-Learning.

The first component, Learning about Atlanta Settings introduces students to Atlanta and its communities through walking tours and observation exercises. Students quickly become familiar with the downtown environment and its relationship to Georgia State. The second component, Learning from Atlanta Systems, provides opportunities to learn further about economics, education, health care, legal, political, and social topics by making structural connections to Atlanta through site visits to urban facilities. For example, students make court visits and write journal reports. Additionally, students make connections between current issues and the city of Atlanta by interviewing system leaders. When students participate in the third component, Learning with Atlanta Communities, they engage with diverse communities through activities such as interviews, action research, fieldwork, or short-term community service with nonprofit agencies. Finally, the last component of the continuum of engagement, Learning by Atlanta Service-Learning, involves Georgia State students with the greater Atlanta community through long-term service-learning activities connected to learning objectives of a specific course.

A full-time academic coordinator, who collaborates with faculty, helping them design and develop initiatives, staffs the Office of Atlanta-Based Learning. This full-time coordinator, who reports to the assistant vice-president for recruitment and retention, is responsible for (a) conducting classroom presentations and reflection exercises, (b) meeting with faculty and academic departments to discuss integration of Atlanta-Based Learning into classes, (c) researching community organizations and Atlanta sites appropriate for a particular academic discipline, (d) meeting with students to assist with site selections, (e) hosting faculty development opportunities and training for using the initiative as engaged learning pedagogy, and (f) providing supplemental readings and resources involving service-learning and civic engagement.

The Law and Society Freshman Learning Community, under the direction of Nancy R. Mansfield, is a successful example of integrating Atlanta-Based Learning in the classroom. Faculty teaching linked courses within this learning community chose "Affirmative Action in Higher Education and the Workplace" as a theme for the semester. Through the GSU 1010: New Student Orientation course, Mansfield linked law/ethics/political theory, rhetoric, writing assignments, community activities, and research with the affirmative action theme. Her students also participated in moot court group activities. By the end of the semester, students critically examined the legal and ethical aspects of segregation, integration, and affirmative action in higher education and the workplace. Linked courses included New Student Orientation, English Composition, Great Questions of Philosophy, American Government, and Math Modeling.

Students participated in a walking tour of Georgia State University to become familiar with the campus and the university's role in the Atlanta community. A tour of Georgia State's nationally ranked College of Law was a highlight. To learn from Atlanta systems, students toured the historic Auburn Avenue District, less than a half mile from campus. Students enjoyed lunch at the Auburn Avenue Curb Market, visited the Dr. Martin Luther King, Jr. Visitors Center, Historic Ebenezer Baptist Church, and Dr. King's birth site. Through site visits, students learned about the history of Atlanta and the critical role of Auburn Avenue in the life of Dr. King and the Civil Rights Movement.

To learn with Atlanta communities, Dr. Mansfield invited local experts to participate in a panel discussion and interviews, sharing their knowledge and experiences with affirmative action. Students researched background information and prepared questions for interviews with a faculty member from the Department of African American Studies, an attorney, and an assistant director of affirmative action from human resources. Finally, students considered service and professional opportunities in the legal field to fulfill their Learning by Atlanta Service-Learning component.

At the conclusion of the semester, student groups completed multi-media projects and reflection papers that integrated course content including video footage that incorporated dialogue from the expert interviews and student impressions of diversity and affirmative action, a comparative analysis of newspaper articles on affirmative action in the 1970s and today, and PowerPoint presentations with photos. The impact of the experiential learning became even more apparent as student groups dedicated their presentations to the legacy of Rosa Parks who died during the semester.

Participation in academic courses that include an Atlanta-Based Learning component gives students meaningful opportunities to experience community and civic engagement linked to their academic interests or major. In turn, faculty provide varied methods of instruction and opportunities for engaged learning. The continuum of engagement offers a unique framework that allows individual students, or an entire class, to be involved with some or all of the components of Atlanta-Based Learning. Students have many opportunities to participate in various forms of engagement: internships, civic practicums, community service projects, and service-learning activities.

Research Design

Two learning outcomes, one for faculty who instruct in the Freshmen Learning Communities (FLC) and one for their students, were assessed: (a) whether faculty who included Atlanta-Based Learning activities in their classes found it beneficial to their course and (b) whether students felt connected to Georgia State University and the Atlanta community as a result of Atlanta-Based Learning activities in their classes. We assessed each outcome by examining faculty and student participation in Atlanta-Based Learning, the types of activities in the classes according to the continuum of engagement, and what was learned from the experience. Additional issues addressed included whether or not Atlanta-Based Learning affected first-year student leadership, interpersonal skills, faculty and student relationships, and awareness of community issues in the first year. At the beginning of the 2006 spring semester, faculty and students who participated in Atlanta-Based Learning were invited via e-mail to complete an online survey to assess their fall 2005 experience. Two separate online surveys were created.

Effectiveness indicators and criteria for success for both outcomes were identified. For the first outcome (whether or not faculty who included Atlanta-Based Learning in their classes found it beneficial to their course), indicators of effectiveness included the number of FLCs that included Atlanta-Based Learning in their syllabi, the percentage or number of each Atlanta-Based Learning component included in FLCs, and faculty perceptions that Atlanta-Based Learning was a positive addition to their course. Success would be determined when at least 75% of the FLCs in fall 2005 included Atlanta-Based Learning activities in their syllabi, and whether at least two out of the four components of the Atlanta-Based Learning continuum were included in each FLC. Success would finally be determined if 50% of faculty surveyed felt that Atlanta-Based Learning was a positive addition to their course.

For our second outcome (students felt connected to Georgia State University and the Atlanta community through Atlanta-Based Learning activities in their classes), indicators of effectiveness included the number of FLC students who felt connected to Georgia State University and the larger community after participating in Atlanta-Based Learning activities in their classes. Success would be determined if at least 50% of students surveyed agreed that they felt connected to Georgia State University through Atlanta-Based Learning, and if at least 50% of students surveyed agreed that they felt connected to the community through Atlanta-Based Learning activities.

Findings

Results showed that 71% of the FLCs in fall 2005 included Atlanta-Based Learning in their classes. Faculty who responded to the online survey strongly agreed that Atlanta-Based Learning was a positive addition to their course. More than half mentioned that they strongly agreed that Atlanta-Based Learning activities were beneficial to their students, and that they themselves learned something new about the community. Additionally, 62% of the FLCs included at least two components of the continuum.

The student survey results showed that of the 93 students who responded to the survey, 44.1% agreed that the Atlanta-Based Learning experience helped them to feel more connected to the community, while 45.7% agreed that it helped them feel connected to Georgia State University. Additionally, students stated that the program enhanced their leadership skills, and they developed knowledge and ideas based on "real-world" experience. Almost half of the students surveyed also mentioned that activities and corresponding group projects taught them the importance of working in groups, and that they became more comfortable in an environment different from their own.

Conclusions

Similar to other institutions, the process of intentionally integrating community engagement and service-learning into courses presents many challenges. These challenges include how to involve faculty, how to make Atlanta-Based Learning activities relevant, how to address time and resources, and how to recognize faculty through release time or benefits. Despite these hurdles, institutionalization of the program is improving. The appointment of a full-time academic coordinator to assist faculty provides needed support, and the creation of a faculty associate program devoted to the office will increase outreach across campus.

Several improvements have been made since the program's inception. First, the university requires Atlanta-Based Learning activities for all Freshmen Learning Communities. Second, faculty who integrate courses and include the third and fourth component of the continuum in their classes are eligible for a $2,000 stipend awarded through a peer-reviewed application process. Finally, we have found that given the opportunity to understand the Atlanta-Based Learning program and to experience extraordinary examples of work from past classes, faculty will integrate the program into their courses on an ad hoc basis. Faculty members in various academic disciplines are engaging their students in community activities, but may not be addressing them as Atlanta-Based Learning activities.

For students, a critical component involves making activities engaging and directly applicable to their academic interest. While some students found their projects meaningful and made the connection between Atlanta-Based Learning issues and their academic work, others completed their projects simply to fulfill their class requirement.

Atlanta-Based Learning's continuum of engagement is flexible and relatively easy to implement. To execute a similar program at another institution, participants must recognize and share the commitment to engaged learning. Collaboration across departments and divisions is important, as well.

The encouragement of faculty best practices, promotion of success in the classroom, and engagement of students and faculty in the classroom and the community underpin Atlanta-Based Learning. The end result is a successful program that incorporates a variety of teaching and learning methods and that connects the university with its larger community.

Primary Contributor

Jean So
Manager of the Welcome Center
Former Program Development Officer for Atlanta-Based Learning
Georgia State University
P.O. Box 3999
Atlanta, GA 30302-3999
Phone: 404-651-3900
E-mail: jeanso@gsu.edu

Additional Contributors

Nancy R. Mansfield
Associate Professor of Legal Studies

Millersville University

Institution Profile

Millersville, PA
Public, Four-Year
Civic Engagement and
Service-Learning

Editors' Notes

In response to concerns about student adjustment to Millersville University, faculty and staff implemented an integrated, living-learning community with three courses, coordinated through the first-year seminar (University 101), which links in- and out-of-class experiences both on-campus and in the community. Using a comprehensive planning and implementation process involving multiple stakeholders, a mixed-design approach to evidence, and a commitment to ongoing oversight, students benefit on multiple levels and reveal higher levels of engagement both with the university and the community.

The Institution

Millersville University, a regional, comprehensive, public university, is one of the 14 state-owned institutions of higher education comprising Pennsylvania's State System of Higher Education. Located in Lancaster County, Pennsylvania, the university enrolls approximately 7,000 undergraduate and 1,000 graduate students, with more than 70% of them full-time undergraduates. The student body is 60% female, one in six is at least 25 years of age, and 11% represent ethnic minority populations (African American 6.3%, Hispanic 2.7%, Asian 1.7%, multiracial 0.2%, and Native American 0.1%). More than 50% of undergraduate students live in either campus-owned or campus-related housing (privately owned student housing immediately adjacent to campus).

Description of the Initiative

Millersville faculty and staff designed and implemented a holistic living-learning community in fall 2001 in response to concerns about student adjustment to the university. This community inclues three courses in which all students are enrolled, a residential experience that includes special programming linked with a first-year seminar, and related requirements (e.g., service-learning, attendance at cocurricular cultural and educational events, and participation in extracurricular activities) designed to foster student adjustment to college and full engagement with university life. Piloted exclusively for students undecided about a major, 40% of eligible students chose to participate in the first several years of implementation.

The living-learning community is coordinated through the first-year seminar, University 101, a one-semester, one-hour, graded, elective course. Predominantly an extended orientation course for exploratory students, it serves as the academic foundation for the living-learning community and is linked with two other courses (either an English composition or communications course and another general education course) to create an integrating theme (e.g., an earth science course, English composition, and University 101 that embraces an "Earth, Wind, and Fire" theme). The seminar has 23 to 25 students in each section and is taught by university faculty, who serve as the students' academic advisors. Faculty are assisted in the seminar by peer mentors who reside with the first-year students in the residence hall. Peer mentors play a pivotal role in facilitating transition by assisting with fulfillment of seminar objectives, providing programs within residence halls on academic and social success, and serving as role models for these exploratory students. They facilitate student attendance at extracurricular and cocurricular events and participation in an all-community service-learning experience, which are key components of the seminar requirements and are designed to facilitate community building and student engagement with the university.

As an outgrowth of the phenomenal success of the living-learning communities, both in terms of student engagement with university life and with improved second-year retention data, the faculty, who are in the midst of general education review, have begun experimenting with a three-credit, content-based first-year seminar, University 179. This approach builds upon the objectives and intent of University 101 but has expanded academic expectations for students. Also, more living-learning communities are being provided for students in selected majors.

A unique feature of both the one-credit and three-credit seminars is the introduction to civic engagement through problem-based learning exercises and service-learning that engages students in situations they may experience either on the college campus or in the surrounding community. Primary course goals include (a) demonstrating strengthened inquiry, research, and information literacy skills; (b) understanding and demonstrating tolerance for the relativity and plurality of human values and beliefs; and (c) reflecting upon the importance of civic responsibility as a vital component of a liberal arts education.

The intended outcome is to provide students with exposure to understanding the importance of civic responsibility early in their university careers in the expectation that early involvement will foster a deepening awareness of and commitment to involved citizenship.

University executive leadership provided initial impetus for the emphasis on civic engagement and the enhancement of service-learning. As a public university, Millersville's mission is to prepare graduates to fully contribute to society. The university has joined with other American Association of State Colleges and Universities (AASCU) institutions and *The New York Times* in the American Democracy Project and is committed to providing students with experiences where they address issues and challenges confronted by the larger community. Concurrent with implementation of living-learning communities, service-learning was identified as a major vehicle by which students are immersed in community-based experiences that expand their understanding of problems facing our society that are frequently identified in course content (e.g., the plight of the homeless, inequities in public education, environmental challenges). Through reflection on their participation in these experiences, students gain increased understanding of their respective roles as citizens in a diverse world.

Service-learning is coordinated through the Office of Community and Academic Partnerships (CAP), which also coordinates cooperative education and internship experiences on campus. CAP staff members work with the faculty in developing service-learning activities within the seminars early in September. Facilitated reflection is built into the program at three key points: (a) preceding the service-learning experience; (b) immediately following the experience; and (c) in class, through class discussion and personal journal reflections.

FYE students, peer mentors, and faculty participate in the United Way of Lancaster County's Day of Caring and provide service to the community as part of United Way work teams. The United Way represents more than 50 nonprofit community service organizations, and the Day of Caring is designed to bring together people from all sectors of the community in providing needed services. This approach stimulates a cross-cultural commitment to community service and energizes people from all over the county. Students benefit not only through their participation as a class cohort in a service project, but as part of a well-coordinated, integrated community effort. Lancaster County's Day of Caring is the largest in the country, with more than 3,000 volunteers working together to improve the community.

Day of Caring activities start with a university-sponsored breakfast and send-off where students, faculty, and peer mentors gain greater appreciation of the day's events. Students then travel to their respective worksites, which relate to their seminar themes (e.g., biology majors work on a greenhouse project, students studying homelessness work at a homeless shelter, students considering a degree in education work in area schools). Following the event, students attend the United Way picnic, bringing together community and university volunteers. Subsequent assignments—including portfolios, i-movies, and journal entries—foster deep reflection and are supplemented with class discussions on the value of civic engagement.

Subsequent service-learning and voluntary community service opportunities are provided throughout the students' overall educational experiences at Millersville. Growth in student involvement in service-learning has been exponential. In 2000-01, 166 students provided 7,047 hours of service-learning to 54 organizations; in 2005-06, more than 2,600 students provided 114,664 hours of service-learning to more than 250 community agencies. Inclusion of this experience within the first-year seminar has been instrumental in fostering this civic engagement agenda.

Research Design

Both quantitative and qualitative analyses were used to determine the effectiveness of service-learning within the first-year seminar. As we designed this entering experience, we were particularly concerned with students' overall recognition of the value of civic engagement, their participation in such an experience as contrasted with students who were not enrolled in a seminar, and their involvement in other service activities beyond those required as part of a class assignment. Millersville University has been an active participant in the National Survey of Student Engagement (NSSE), and we had been reviewing all items within the instrument, but particularly those items that addressed service-learning and related matters. These benchmarked findings have been integral to the university's commitment to institutional quality, and data have provided evidence of areas of success as well as areas for improvement.

In bringing a recommendation on the formal adoption of the seminar course forward to the Faculty Senate, it was requested that we provide interim data in fall 2004. An in-house survey was developed and administered in December to determine student responses to quantitative and qualitative prompts regarding transition to college life. Students provided demographic information and responded to such open-ended items as:

- Were you involved in any service-learning activities?
- If yes, what did you do?
- How well did you like your service-learning experience?

Within the survey instrument, several short-answer statements were tailored for consistency with NSSE so that we could compare findings with both prior and a planned 2005 administration of the national survey.

Student journal entries were also evaluated to determine additional qualitative findings. Journal prompts included:

- Please reflect on your experience with service-learning. How does giving back to the community have the potential to change who you are, both today and in the future?
- How could this experience change the lives of others?

Research Findings

The fall 2004 in-house survey was provided electronically to 1,488 first-year students. A total of 333 students responded; 84 of whom were FYE students. The remaining 249 students were not.

Statistically significant differences ($p < .05$) were found between participants and nonparticipants on a number of questions, with FYE students reporting more positive responses on the following items:

- Worked with faculty members on activities outside of class
- Participated in a community-based project as part of a course
- Participated in community service or volunteer work outside of class

In addition, students rated their service-learning experiences more positively. FYE students rated the experience as good (27.03%) or excellent (18.92%) as contrasted with nonparticipants (good = 16.84%, excellent = 11.05%).

Follow-up analyses of the 2005 NSSE means comparison report provided evidence that this initiative has had a positive impact, not only among first-year students but among senior students as well. It should be noted that seniors responding to the 2005 NSSE entered in the fall of 2001, the first year we began our pilot study. Selected findings are in Table 1.

Table 1
2005 National Survey of Student Engagement Means Comparison Regarding Community Service

	First-Year Students		Senior-Year Students	
	Millersville	Peer institutions	Millersville	Peer institutions
Academic and intellectual experience (e.g., community-based project as part of course)	1.56*	1.45	1.79	1.73
Enriching educational experiences (e.g., community service or volunteer work)	.39	.34	.66**	.57
Educational and personal growth (e.g., contributing to the welfare of your community)	2.37	2.24*	2.43	2.36

*$p < .05$, **$p < .01$

Findings provide preliminary evidence that emphasis on service-learning may impact students beyond the duration of their first-year experience. Also, the comparison analyses of student responses with selected peer institution students validate the university's emphasis on these experiences. Student journal entries provide additional evidence of the value of these experiences.

"Having this experience allowed me to get to know my seminar class in a more personal way. Working to clean up the playground gave me a sense of pride. It was nice to think we were doing something for the children."

"I know that every time I help others I am also helping myself."

"When we first were told about this assignment, I wasn't all that excited. After I had a chance to see the difference we could make in one morning, I felt good about myself and decided it was a good thing after all."

" I wouldn't mind doing this again. It was fun and worthwhile."

" I never thought about the impact I could have on someone else's life. It meant a lot to me to have the opportunity to interact with my class in this way. I think all students should have a chance to do this. Seeing people from the community working together was neat."

"I think when we do this for others it may help them think about doing something for someone else. Like in the movie we saw. A kind of ripple effect."

Conclusions

As these findings indicate, the inclusion of service-learning as an integral part of the first-year seminar has yielded some very positive results, both in qualitative and quantitative assessments. Campus surveys provide evidence that participating students rate the experience more positively than do nonparticipants. NSSE results provide support for the continued inclusion of service-learning in programs for entering university students, as both first-year and senior students rate the experiences higher than students at selected peer institutions, with several findings demonstrating significant differences.

What Worked Well at Millersville

The overall experience was a resounding success. In particular, coordinating the first-year experience with a county-wide United Way initiative early in the semester afforded students an engagement experience not only with fellow classmates, but with a wide range of individuals throughout the county, stressing the importance of such initiatives.

Critical Elements

A university administration committed to the principles of civic engagement and support of service-learning is vital to its success. In addition, the assumption of coordination efforts by the CAP office on campus assured implementation. Without the effort of CAP staff, this would have been extremely difficult, if not impossible, to provide.

Lessons Learned

Faculty buy-in is necessary, but not always immediate. We struggled at first with getting some seminar faculty on board with the service-learning effort. It is important to demonstrate to faculty the beneficial outcomes associated with service-learning. Service-learning for the sake of service-learning and preparing responsible citizens may be viewed as too obscure. You must be able to demonstrate that students understand certain concepts better, such as homelessness and the plight of the disenfranchised, as a result of participating in service experiments.

Lessons other campuses can learn from our work include:

- Build support for service-learning across the university with administrators and faculty. Have an organized staff, who are committed to these efforts, provide the needed assistance, and support implementation.
- Situate the experience within a context for greater student and staff participation. It enhances team-building and early engagement with varied aspects of university life. Being

part of a larger community effort stresses the value of such efforts early in the students' learning experience.

- Work with the faculty to address their concerns about relevance of these experiences and ensure that concerns about curricular integrity are addressed.
- Use good assessment strategies and, in particular, seek validation through national benchmarked surveys. NSSE analyses and good data have been vital in advancing this effort on our campus.

Service-learning, occurring early in students' college careers, has facilitated successful transition and fostered understanding of civic engagement. Continued efforts to broaden this learning experience are warranted by findings at this time.

Primary Contributor

Linda L. McDowell, Professor
Coordinator, Freshman Year Experience
Millersville University
P.O. Box 1002
Millersville, PA 17551-0302
Phone: 717-871-2388
E-mail: Linda.mcdowell@millersville.edu

Additional Contributors

Carol Y. Phillips
Administrator Emerita

Texas A&M-Corpus Christi

Institution Profile

Corpus Christi, TX
Public, Four-Year
Civic Engagement and
Service Learning

Editors' Notes

Texas A&M-Corpus Christi has a broad institutional commitment to learning communities. A coalition of faculty in English, political science, and communications has made a commitment to work on the common learning theme of the First Amendment, with broader themes such as community, civility in discourse, and civic responsibility. The project operates within the university's larger involvement in the American Democracy Project of the American Association of State Colleges and Universities. While integration of objectives necessitates some compromise of individual faculty autonomy, outcomes are assessed not only across the learning community but also within specific disciplinary and course objectives. Multiple evaluations are used, including participation in national benchmarking studies.

The Institution

Texas A&M University-Corpus Christi (TAMU-CC) is located in Corpus Christi, Texas, on the coast of the Gulf of Mexico. It is a four-year, regional public institution, which serves primarily commuter students. A spring 2006 Park & Ride Survey reported that about 88% students commuted daily (Hardin). In fall 2005, the student population totaled 8,365 students comprised of 62% women and 38% men (Student Enrollment Factbook); first-year student enrollment totaled approximately 1,350 students. TAMU-CC is a Hispanic-Serving Institution, with a significant Latino/a population (37.6%). Whites comprise a slight majority of the student population (54.6%). Other ethnic groups are minimally represented: 3.6% African American, 2.2% Asian American, 1.3% international, and 0.7% Native American.

Description of the Initiative

Civic Engagement as a Curricular Initiative

Faculty participate in the American Democracy Project (ADP) for three overlapping reasons: institutional mission, personal commitment, and research supporting civic engagement. Preparing students "for lifelong learning and for responsible participation in the global community" is a part of our institutional mission (TAMU-CC, 2003). Many faculty recognize the importance, especially for students from historically under-represented groups, of the development of intellectual understandings of civic engagement. In addition, research shows that student interest and participation in politics and community service are in a state of decline (Colby, Ehrlich, Beaumont, & Stephens, 2003). This decline highlights the importance of developing in students a combination of knowledge, skills, values, and motivation so they are able to make informed judgments (Ehrlich, 2000).

Since spring 2003, we have used the ADP to foster civic engagement with first-year students, all of whom are enrolled in the First Year Learning Communities Program (FYLCP). The FYLCP links the two semesters of English composition; two semesters of critical thinking-focused, discussion-based seminar; and one or two large lecture courses, such as American history or American government. Communication classes are significant additions to many students' first-year experience. We have specifically incorporated First Amendment themes for two academic years, 2005-2006 and 2006-2007, to encourage intellectual and experiential civic engagement. This case study focuses on ways to incorporate the theme of civic engagement into the curriculum of three disciplinary areas: English composition, political science, and speech/communication.

First Amendment in the First-Year Learning Communities Program

In composition, students and teachers discussed, read, and wrote about First Amendment freedoms. Writing teachers collaborated with reference librarians to develop a long list of academically reliable web sites. They served our goals by exposing our students to multiple perspectives and requiring them to read and understand the arguments of others. The articles were intellectually challenging and civically engaging. Students are considered "apprentices" in academic discourse, and the program moves them toward fuller participation in that discourse through staged writing tasks.

The TAMU-CC writing assignment sequence begins with a prompt that asks students to describe their home communities and what "citizenship" looked like in those communities. Teachers interpreted "communities" in the sense of "discourse communities," not just as physical, civic locations, but also as groups such as families, high schools, or civic associations, in which patterns of behavior and speech define the identity of participants. "Citizenship" was a term teachers and students defined collaboratively, as it applied to the students' participation in these communities. As an extension of these explorations, we asked students how the First Amendment themes were enacted and about the various forms of citizenship that existed in their experiences.

The second writing assignment asked students to identify a social issue that interested them; teachers encouraged students to find an issue connected to their communities and form(s) of citizenship. Students objectively presented at least three perspectives on these social issues. In the third assignment, students made multimedia arguments for action at an all-day first-year celebration event. These presentations modeled the kinds of civic literacy and agency promoted by the ADP.

Civic Engagement and Political Science

Introductory political science courses have also been influenced by the ADP's civic engagement emphasis, especially those involved in the learning communities. The introductory classes have tried to encourage civic engagement by promoting intellectual engagement, the acquisition of information, and the understanding of its importance through regular use of *The New York Times*. Each week, students were expected to find two articles, one that they found "interesting," and one that was "important." For each, students were instructed to write a one-paragraph critical response. In the learning community classes, these articles were often the source of discussion and debate. In conjunction with the First Amendment themes over the past semesters, *The New York Times* was a source of information for students' papers and presentations and has been especially useful in regard to freedom of speech issues. In large lecture classes, the paper was used as a reference point, and students were encouraged to comment on and critique the decisions of politicians. The current "topic of the day" was used to illuminate and enliven textbook concepts and historical examples, which assisted students in making connections. Finally, the political science faculty has used their ties to the community to bring in speakers to discuss issues ranging from the local to international. In preparation for meeting with these speakers, students were encouraged to follow related issues in *The New York Times*.

Media Literacy and Public Competency in Communication

The Student Civic Engagement and Media Literacy curricular initiative was centered in a communication course with a media literacy emphasis. This civic engagement initiative focused on taking on a problem involving media competency and public health. The students were challenged to integrate curricular materials into practice in their everyday lives. To help facilitate the learning objectives, students, in teams of five, were required to apply critical approaches to the media by developing a media literacy workshop (30-45 minutes) to present at junior high and high schools, literacy councils, and other available nonprofit organizations. Based on the age group and focus of the given audience, each media literacy workshop varied and demanded the use of different levels of written and oral communication skills. For example, the media literacy workshops presented to junior high and high school students focused on topics such as relationships and dating as presented in popular media (e.g., MTV's *The Real World*). In the case of adult learners, student media literacy workshops focused on prescription drug advertising (e.g., diet pills and Viagra).

During one semester, students in this course made presentations to more than 200 students at local junior high and high schools. Another team made presentations to 40 Latino adult learners who had mastered English as a second language but needed to improve their critical thinking and media analysis skills. The learning environment outside the classroom encouraged teachers to innovate and students to connect course content, community, and self (Wahl & Edwards, 2006; Wahl & Quintanilla, 2005). Finally, in the communication class, the public presentation directly involved the community, linking curricular activities to civic engagement.

Research Design

Due to the interdisciplinary nature of our ADP program, multiple research methods were used to assess the program. In English courses, we asked a sample of 100 students from four classes, all of whom completed the writing sequence described above, to read common texts. Those who participated in history and sociology learning communities responded to the question, "What does the First Amendment mean to you?" At the First-Year Celebration, we interviewed students about their research projects, the First Amendment, and their learning over the course of the semester. In the political science class, more traditional methods were used, typically pre-post assessments and attitudinal surveys. A pre-post test over basic political knowledge was given to students in the learning communities, which involved more than 300 students. A later, more systematic, study of students was conducted, which compared a learning community class that used *The New York Times* with a learning community class and nonlearning community class that did not use the paper (282 students were involved in this second survey). A third survey asked approximately 500 students to rate their levels of engagement in the classroom, cocurricular activities, and nonschool related volunteer activities (i.e., political, social, religious, and cultural). The survey also queried students about what motivated them to become civically engaged using an affective, obligatory, and instrumental framework.

In the communication class, we wanted to test whether media literacy workshops presented by the communication students at junior high and high schools, literacy councils, and other nonprofit organizations would support previous research that contended that civic engagement benefits student learning and social development (Corbett & Kendall, 1999; Eyler, 2000; Eyler & Giles, 1999). We relied on reflective statements given by students at the end of the semester for a portion of our research. We also had approximately 125 students participate in more formal class assessments, specifically a set of post-interviews that were done to trace the impact of the specific activity.

Findings

These three curricular initiatives highlighted our efforts to engage students, and our findings are based upon discipline-specific methods. In English, we reviewed the written responses to our research question about the meaning of the First Amendment. Students demonstrated a more concrete and complex understanding of First Amendment rights and were more likely to personalize that understanding and connect it to their own situations and communities. Students claimed: "I can have a voice and my opinion and not die for it." and "I am able to say what I want, practice whatever religion I want." Interviews with students regarding their research, which included several contemporary topics (e.g., slavery in the Sudan, PETA, and the Patriot Act), demonstrated students' growing awareness of, and engagement in, a variety of perspectives and beliefs.

In political science, we discovered that classroom performance has been enhanced by the use of *The New York Times*. In the introductory courses, the pre-post tests showed that classes that used the newspaper had a four percentage point increase in scores, attributable solely to reading the newspaper. The comparative survey showed that students in the learning community class using *The New York Times* were more likely to stay current with the news and find the news important, more likely to find the class material relevant, and had a more positive attitude toward the class. Finally, students also had more positive attitudes toward civic engagement, suggesting that the students discovered that they were part of a larger community (Huerta & Jozwiak, in press). Our major survey of engagement showed that even our initial efforts at encouraging civic engagement have had a positive impact on our first-year students (Jorgensen, Jozwiak, & Huerta, 2006).

For communication, the response to the civic engagement project has been extremely positive both on the part of the students and the community. From the activity, specific data retrieved during and after the media literacy project, we found that students and the professor thought about learning in a different way as course content was connected to a community concern about media literacy (Wahl & Edwards, 2006). On course assessments, the students rated their community engagements experiences "very worthwhile." On written evaluations, students noted several positive experiences about this project. For example, one student commented that this project provided a "lot of hands-on experience. We actually got to put our class work into action." Another student remarked about feeling as though they "made a personal contribution to the community." During follow-up interviews, each of the community organizations emphasized high levels of satisfaction with the media literacy workshops. In fact, one of the junior high teachers wrote, "My students and I have been talking about your students' presentations all week. Beyond the media literacy workshop, this was a great forum for college students to set an example for the youngsters. I hope we can continue this partnership."

Conclusions

We are continuing to integrate the ADP into our campus culture with faculty, students, and staff members stepping forward to celebrate civic engagement on our campus and in the community. For other institutions considering adopting an ADP project, we would make recommendations at the faculty and institutional level. In order to build successful experiences at the classroom level, instructor planning and reflecting is absolutely necessary. Consciously thinking about goals is a must. Assigning classroom prompts, and then giving students a wide variety of materials to work with is essential. The willingness to work toward classroom activities and writing projects that encourage critical student reflection is paramount. Success also requires cooperation among faculty who are willing to give up some autonomy in order to achieve larger goals. It also means working well with other entities on campus, such as the library. Institutions should also remember that assessing engagement can be accomplished using many different measures that will appeal to various faculty and administrative agendas and methods.

In terms of recommendations for other institutions seeking to replicate or adapt our efforts, we believe the upper administration must be invested in the ADP vision. At TAMU-CC, the administration has been supportive of the ADP. At the same time, it has been challenging to keep the momentum going with the arrival of new university leadership. Thus, institutions interested in implementing the ADP must focus on internal communication and advocate for institutional support during any administrative change. Further, campuses should ensure the ADP is connected to the institutional strategic plan, vision, and mission.

In the upcoming years, we plan to coordinate these curricular efforts with speakers, writing and speech contests, and other special events. We plan to coordinate further with our research office to use both the National Survey of Student Engagement (NSSE) and internal surveys to measure the effectiveness of curricular and cocurricular efforts to engage students in community and citizenship issues. While we have found that the success of the ADP has been a process of constant adjustment and the compromise of competing visions, it continues to provide a coordinating framework upon which our interdisciplinary efforts can be built.

References

Colby, A., Ehrlich, T., Beaumont, E., & Stephens, J. (2003). *Educating citizens: Preparing America's undergraduates for lives of moral and civic responsibility*. San Francisco: Jossey-Bass.

Corbett, J. B., & Kendall, A. R. (1999). Evaluating service-learning in the communication discipline. *Journalism and Mass Communication Educator, 53*, 66-76.

Ehrlich, T. (2000). *Civic responsibility and higher education*. Phoenix, AZ: Oryx Press.

Eyler, J. S. (2000). What do we need to know about the impact of service-learning on student learning? *Michigan Journal of Community Service-learning, 4*, 5-15.

Eyler, J. S., & Giles, D. (1999). *Where's the learning in service-learning?* San Francisco: Jossey-Bass.

Hardin, B. (2006). Park and ride survey. Office of Planning & Institutional Effectiveness Texas A&M University-Corpus Christi.

Huerta C., & Jozwiak J. (in press). Developing civic engagement in general education political science. *Journal of Political Science Education*.

Jorgensen, D., Jozwiak, J., & Huerta, C. (2006). Assessing the multiple dimensions of student civic engagement: A preliminary test of an ADP survey instrument. In J. Perry & S. Jones (Eds.), *Quick hits for educating citizens: Successful strategies by award-winning teachers* (pp. 71-78). Bloomington: Indiana University Press.

Student Enrollment Factbook. (2005). Office of Planning & Institutional Effectiveness Texas A&M University-Corpus Christi. Retrieved May 1, 2006, from http://pie.tamucc.edu/

Texas A&M Universisty-Corpus Christi. (2003). Institutional vision, mission, principles, goals. (2003). Office of the Provost. Retrieved February 12, 2007, from http://www.tamucc.edu/provost/mission/index.html

Tyner, K. (1998). *Literacy in a digital world: Teaching and learning in the age of information*. Mahwah, NJ: Lawrence Erlbaum.

Wahl, S. T., & Edwards, C. (2006). Enacting a pragmatist educational metaphysic through civic engagement in the basic media studies communication course. *Basic Communication Course Annual, 18*, 148-173.

Wahl, S. T., & Quintanilla, K. M. (2005). Student civic engagement and media literacy. *Texas Speech Communication Journal, 30*(1), 89-91.

Primary Contributor

Joseph Jozwiak
Associate Professor of Political Science
Texas A&M-Corpus Christi
6300 Ocean Drive
Corpus Christi, TX 78412-5812
Phone: 361-825-5997
E-mail: joseph.jozwiak@tamucc.edu

Additional Contributors

Susan Wolf Murphy
Assistant Professor of English

Shawn Wahl
Assistant Professor of Communication

Section 2
Early Intervention – Diagnostic Tools

Cuyamaca College

Institution Profile

*El Cajon, CA
Public, Two-Year
Early Intervention -
Diagnostic Tools*

Editors' Notes

While many two-year institutions offer a first-year course directly for students intending to continue their college educations beyond the associate's degree, what is notable about the program offered by Cuyamaca College in California is not only its format (the 56 sections are either online, blended, or traditional face-to-face), but the fact that many of these sections are actually held on the campuses of local high schools, with high school counselors involved in teaching. This three-unit course also has the distinction of being the first college success course accepted as transferable to the University of California and is required for students who come through the guaranteed transfer program for UC San Diego. This initiative represents a true partnership approach to critical transitional points (from high school to a two-year institution to a four-year institution). The research design is built into the oversight of the program and includes multiple measures at multiple capture points.

The Institution

Cuyamaca College is a public community college located in El Cajon, California. It is a commuter college that offers a variety of programs in vocational education, transfer studies, and courses for personal enrichment. Approximately 8,000 students attend Cuyamaca College. Many of these students are part-time students, which makes the full-time equivalent student enrollment 5,183. Each semester, approximately 60% are continuing students, and 40% are new students. Some of these new students are first-time students and others are returning to college after a period of absence from education. No statistics are maintained on first-generation students, although the college has an Educational Opportunity Program for low-income and first-generation students that has approximately 525 students each year. Cuyamaca College has an enrollment of 56% female students and 44% male students. Forty percent of students enrolled in the college are over 25 years of age. Since Cuyamaca College is located near the Mexican border, it has a very diverse population of students with 56% of students in the White, non-Hispanic category, 20% Hispanic, 7% Asian, 6% African American, and 13% listed as other. The White category includes a large number of Iraqi immigrants who live in the area.

Description of the Initiative

Currently at Cuyamaca College, 1,600 students enroll yearly in Personal Development 124 (PDC 124), Lifelong Success. This comprehensive course contains student learning outcomes in the areas of college, career, and lifelong successes. Approximately 50% of these students are first-time students under 20 years of age. This course has been identified as one of the top 15 revenue-producing programs of the college. The college offers 56 sections of this course each year with an average of 28 students per section. Eighteen of these sections have recently been offered on the campuses of local high schools. High school counselors encourage students to enroll in the course as a way to help them understand college expectations, prepare for learning in college, and planning their majors and careers. In most cases, high school counselors are teaching the course on their campus. As the number of high school sections increases, the numbers of young first-time students enrolled in the course are expected to increase.

Using technology in education is identified as a necessary college success skill, and it is used extensively in teaching the course. The course is offered in various format, including online (12 sections), blended or hybrid formats (22 sections), and traditional face-to-face formats (22 sections).

The online courses include personality and vocational assessments, reading material, quizzes offering immediate feedback, discussion boards, e-mail, and instructional videos. With the exception of three online sections for high school students that require an on-campus orientation at the beginning of the semester, the courses are taught completely online. Blended sections are 51% face-to-face and 49% online. Students in the blended class complete assessments, reading materials, quizzes, and journals online. Interactive exercises are completed in the classroom. Traditional face-to-face classes are taught in classrooms with assessments and some course materials posted online.

At the college, this comprehensive three-unit course is recommended for first-time college students, students who are undecided about their majors, and students who are on academic probation. While exact numbers of the above groups of students enrolling in the course are not available, the District Office of Institutional Research has identified these students as high-risk students who have persistence rates below the average of the general population. First-time students are defined as students who have no college credits and are beginning college for the first time. Persistence is defined as students who return the next semester. Students are placed on academic probation if their grade point averages are below 2.0. This course has been offered at the college since 2000, and a similar course was offered from 1990 to 2000.

Although this course is not a requirement for new students, it has excellent enrollment due to several factors:

- The course has a reputation for quality and is recommended by counselors and faculty.
- The course transfers to the California State University system to meet general education requirements.
- It is the first college success course accepted as transferable to the University of California. It is required of students participating in the guaranteed transfer program for the University of California, San Diego.

College success topics prepare students for lifelong learning in this and future courses. Students begin by exploring their reasons for attending college and ways to motivate themselves to accomplish future goals. They learn about time management techniques as the steps needed to accomplish these lifetime goals. Students explore their learning style and identify the learning strategies that work best for them. They practice memory techniques and apply these techniques to improve reading comprehension (e.g., the basics of note taking, test preparation, and college writing).

Choice of a college major and career planning are some of the most important outcomes of the course. Career success topics begin with an assessment of personality types and related careers. Based on these personal assessments, students explore careers that match their personal strengths. Students also assess their values and vocational interests. Career assessment is followed by educational planning to complete general education requirements, preparation for the major, and the requirements needed to transfer to four-year universities.

Lifelong success topics prepare students for future success in education, the workplace, and their personal lives. Building on their knowledge of personality type, students increase their understanding of good communication techniques and building good relationships. The critical and creative thinking topics include identifying fallacies in reasoning, developing the critical thinking process, and applying creativity techniques to generate ideas for problem resolution. Students practice critical and creative thinking techniques by applying them to current issues. Students are encouraged to maintain a healthy lifestyle over a lifetime by creating a wellness plan that includes nutrition, exercise, proper sleep, relaxation, and the avoidance of addictions. Students also examine issues related to the appreciation of diversity. Lastly, students examine topics related to positive thinking and lifetime happiness.

The complete program review, detailed course outline with student learning objectives, and summaries of additional research are available by clicking on faculty resources at www.cuyamaca. edu/collegesuccess.

Research Design

Every five years, academic programs anad their cost effectiveness are reviewed. Some key questions asked about this course include:

- Does Personal Development 124, Lifelong Success (PDC 124) increase persistence in college?
- Does PDC 124 help students improve their confidence in their academic skills?
- Does PDC 124 help students choose a major?
- What is the level of student satisfaction with the course?

A comparison was made of persistence rates of all students attending Cuyamaca College, all students who enroll in PDC 124, and all students who successfully complete PDC 124. The District Office of Institutional Research, Planning, and Academic Services provided data for this comparison. Student satisfaction and other relevant information were obtained by surveying 198 students enrolled in PDC 124 during the spring semester, 2003.

Findings

Data were analyzed to show the persistence of students who enrolled in the fall and returned in the spring (2000-2004). The data show a greater persistence rate for students who successfully completed PDC 124. The average persistence rate from fall 2000 to spring 2004 for the entire college was 57.8%. The average persistence rate for all PDC students was 76.1%. The average persistence rate for students who successfully completed PDC 124 during the same period was 85.4%, a 26.7% increase over the rates for all students attending the college. The last two program reviews completed over a period of 10 years have shown a consistent increase in persistence rates for students successfully completing PDC 124.

The same persistence data were analyzed for first-time students since they represent approximately half of the students who enroll in PDC 124. From fall 2000 to spring 2004, an average of 63% of first-time Cuyamaca College students who enrolled in the fall returned for the spring. The data shows a greater persistence rate for first-time students who successfully completed PDC 124. For first-time students who successfully completed PDC 124, an average of 88.9% of students returned for the spring semester, an increase of 25.9%.

During the spring semester 2003, a survey was administered to 198 students enrolled in PDC 124. Students' perceptions of the course were generally positive with

- 62% of students saying the course helped them feel more confident about their academic skills

- 72% believing the course would help them improve their grades
- 52% believing that the course was helpful in making a career choice, if they had not already made that decision
- 88% of students giving PDC 124 the highest ratings of very good or good

The program review showed the benefits of offering a comprehensive, three-unit college success course that included a career component. The results of the program review show that students at Cuyamaca College taking and successfully completing PDC 124 have increased persistence by about 27%. The course helped students decide on a major and career and increased their confidence in their academic skills. Students were very satisfied with the course.

Conclusions

Some key elements that contribute to the success of this program include the following:

1. *Transferability.* Students are motivated to enroll in a course that meets graduation requirements and can be transferred to a state university toward a bachelor's degree. The course has been approved as transferable its comprehensive nature and academic rigor. Universities view study skills courses as basic skills courses that are non-transferable. Adding the career and life planning components, led to its acceptance as a transferable course. The academic rigor of a course is also important in gaining acceptance from universities. Appropriate theories are introduced in the course, while keeping the increasing its academic rigor. At the same time, the emphasis remains on practical application.

2. *Career exploration.* Students are motivated to take the course because they need help with career exploration and academic planning. Research completed at Cuyamaca College has shown that students are more likely to persist in their education if they have selected an appropriate major and have a clear academic goal.

3. *Institutional support.* The administration and faculty support the course for many reasons, including steady enrollment and increased student persistence resulting in increased funding for the college.

4. *Counseling support.* Counselors have seen first hand the beneficial results of this course and recommend it during new student orientation and academic planning sessions.

5. *Reputation.* Since the course has been successfully offered in various forms since 1990, there are many former students who have taken the course and recommended it to others. Faculty members understand the benefits of the course and frequently recommend it to their students. Demonstrating how the course supports institutional values related to student success and offers financial advantages for the institution can also enhance the reputation among faculty and administrators.

Primary Contributor

Marsha Fralick
Counselor, Instructor and Personal Development Department Chair
Cuyamaca College
900 Rancho San Diego Parkway
El Cajon, CA 92019-4304
Phone: 619-660-4432
E-mail: marsha.fralick@gcccd.edu

Northern Arizona University

Institution Profile

Flagstaff, AZ
Public, Four-Year
Early Intervention -
Diagnostic Tools

Editors' Notes

What factors contribute to the likelihood of a student's success in college? How accurately does the term "at-risk" reflect the lived experiences of students who enter college for the first time? What interventions work, at what stages, and at what point do at-risk students become less at risk? Not satisfied with the evidence they were collecting or their mechanisms for helping students earlier in the educational process, the faculty and staff at Northern Arizona University engaged in a systematic study of the educational problem. Their integrated approach to identification and intervention is based firmly in the research literature related to predictors of student success, while allowing for individual needs and personal goals.

The Institution

Northern Arizona University, located in Flagstaff, Arizona, is a public four-year institution. It is a residential university with a growing distance learning program, offering courses at multiple statewide sites including a second campus in Yuma, Arizona. The university enrolls approximately 13,000 FTE undergraduates, including roughly 2,100 first-time, full-time, first-year students.

As a residential and public institution, Northern Arizona University's undergraduate student body is 60% female, 40% male, and 24% over 25 years of age (with 2% of first-time, first-year students over 25). The university's ethnic enrollment ($n = 13,252$) includes higher than average percentages of Hispanic (12%) and Native American (7%) students, and lower percentages of African American (2%) and Asian American (2%) students. The majority of students (73%) are White. The remaining distribution includes international students (2%) and students who have not reported their ethnicity (2%).

The best data source the university has for identifying first-generation college students is the Cooperative Institutional Research Program (CIRP) Freshman Survey (Astin, Panos, & Creager, 1966). In the last two years, approximately 35% of students completing the CIRP at New Student Orientation have labeled themselves first-generation college students. Neither parent of these students has completed a bachelor's or higher educational degree.

Description of the Initiative

Our project was developed by a small task force which meets to discuss mechanisms to facilitate first-year student success. The task force is comprised of members from the following areas: Advising/Career Center, faculty, Freshmen Seminar, Native American Student Services, Assessment, Multicultural Student Center, Learning Assistance Centers, and New Student Programs.

The task force was formed to address proactive, intrusive interventions. There was a general feeling that we had the right services and programs, but that students (and, therefore, student services staff) were consuming resources in a "reactive" mode, thus lessening the opportunity for positive impact. Therefore, the keys to our proactive, intrusive intervention mechanism were the ability to predict which students would benefit from which resources and to get those students to access those resources proactively.

Like many campuses, our institutional history includes the implementation and use of various commercially prepared tools for predicting student service needs and their likelihood of success. Drawing from prior experiences, we developed the following understandings to guide our selection and subsequent use of a tool:

- Information (data) gleaned from the administration of a student success tool must be usable by both student services/faculty and students.
- Data must be provided in a user-friendly, accessible format.
- Data must be provided early enough for dissemination and use by both student services and students themselves.
- Results must, in obvious ways, connect students to university resources.
- Different areas of campus must be willing to provide programming to meet the needs identified by the student success tool.

After carefully reviewing our set of "understandings," campus needs, three commercially available products (Bar-On, 2004; Le, Casillas, Robbins, & Langley, 2005; Stratil, 2004), and the pilot of two of the products, we are moving into our third year of project implementation using the Student Readiness Inventory (SRI; Le et al., 2005). Four institutional objectives were developed related to the administration and subsequent consumption of the data from this student success tool:

- Identify early and make direct contact with students who were determined to be at-risk for either failure to persist at the institution or failure to remain in good academic standing.
- Use the information from the tool to match student needs with specific university resources and services.
- Embed profile survey results in our first-yesr seminars to facilitate students' understanding of the connection between their needs and corresponding campus resources.
- Use the composite indices of retention and academic success to build a customized retention prediction equation for our institution.

Our first objective, to identify early and make direct contact with students who were deemed at-risk (either retention or academic success) was met through the use of the composite indices of the SRI. Using the indices, a set of decision-making rules was developed and a "best served" group of students was identified. These students were then invited by different campus offices for one-on-one meetings with an advisor.

Two key challenges of this process were (a) ensuring we did not duplicate efforts by encouraging students to come into more than one office and (b) providing resources that could be embraced by multiple offices. To address the first, representatives on the task force developed a pecking order. That is, in the event that a student had been flagged as a potential participant for multiple programs, we decided which office would conduct outreach to that student in order to share their SRI results. This did not mean that multiple programs did not recruit the student, but it did allow us to assign responsibility for giving back the student's SRI results. In terms of the second challenge, we developed a web site that articulates and crosswalks the student success domains from the SRI instrument with the specific resources, activities, programs, and/or services on our campus. This was particularly helpful because staff members could use it in meetings with students to make referrals, and students, who were now familiar with the web resource, could independently return to the web site later.

Our first objective was met when the identified group of "best served" students (a) met for one-on-one sessions with advisors in the Gateway Student Success Center, (b) were enrolled in the Retention Alert Program, (c) met with peer advisors in the Multicultural Student Center, and/ or (d) visited the Native American Student Services office. All students were provided relevant services by the noted offices as well as referred to other appropriate campus resources.

Our second objective was met by using the information from the instrument to match student needs, as determined by low subscale scores, with specific university resources and services. This intervention involved directly contacting students (e.g., e-mail, postcards) to invite them to access services or participate in events. This was done without explicitly informing students that contact was based on SRI scores. Duplication of contact was deemed appropriate so that, for example, a student who had low scores on the Study Skills scale and on the Social Activity scale would be invited to both study skills workshops and social events.

Specific examples of how this objective was met include identification of students (a) likely to have academic difficulty by the Learning Assistance Center, (b) with low scores on social connectedness by Student Life, Campus Services, and Unions and Student Activities, and (c) with low retention scores and/or low academic success scores by The Gateway Student Success Center. Additionally, students of color with low retention scores were identified by the Multicultural Student Center. Finally, in an effort to engage higher-scoring students who we know can also be at risk of leaving the institution, we used select scale scores to create a list of students who were recruited to leadership positions by Residence Life and New Student Program.

Our third objective was met by including students' SRI profiles in the instructional activities of our first-year seminar courses. Our institution has two seminars, a three-credit study skills course (for underprepared admits), and a one-credit transition to college course. Where the course curriculum already related to specific success domains, student's subscale scores were used as an opportunity for further student reflection and decision making. For example, Goal Striving and General Determination scales were referenced during the course activity on Goal Setting, and the Social Connection and Social Activity scales were referenced when students selected their out-of class experiences. Additionally, the instructors of the study skills seminar met one-on-one with students to review their entire set of results and develop an action plan by selecting university resources and activities relevant to their individual needs. The first-year seminar instructors were able to use the web site of services, articulated with scale domain, to make these referrals.

Our fourth and final approach toward including the tool and its results in first-year programming will be to use the composite indices (retention and academic success), along with behavioral measures of student engagement, retention, and academic performance to build customized retention and performance models for our institution. Longitudinal data including students' academic performance, institutional persistence, and participation in academic and pro-academic social activities are being collected over a two-year period (and are therefore not presented here). We used students' high school academic performance, standardized test scores (e.g., ACT or SAT), and SRI scores to develop predictive models of student success.

Research Design

Programs designed to promote the effective transition of first-year college students abound on campuses in this country and around the world. In our experience, however, many colleges and universities lack a systemic, integrated, and coordinated set of programs. Indeed, that was the challenge on our campus. Thus, the project described in this contribution was designed to bring first-year campus programs and services together around our common focus and better coordinate efforts within that focus.

We began with a review of literature and identified three commercially prepared products aimed at facilitating student success by matching campus support services to subscale scores. The three tools we reviewed were The College Student Inventory (Stratil, 2004), The Student Readiness Inventory (Le et al., 2005) and the Emotional Quotient Inventory (Bar-On, 2004). During the first year of the project, The College Student Inventory was administered to those first-year students who attended New Student Orientation, and during the second year of the project the Student Readiness Inventory (SRI) was administered to all orientation attendees. Part of the reasoning for switching to the SRI was its construction using results from a comprehensive meta-analysis (Robbins, Lauver et al., 2004) and the evidence that the SRI scores are valid predictors of college student outcomes (Gore, 2006; Robbins, Allen, Casillas, Peterson, & Le, 2006).

Given the exploratory nature of our project, we adopted a descriptive approach to evaluating the impact of our efforts. Specifically, we describe the number of students who received referrals or additional services as a result of our project and, when possible, what proportion of students acted on referrals.

More formal tracking methods were used to evaluate student engagement variables. An institutional database is maintained to store student records of participation in enrollment management and student affairs activities such as campus residency, tutoring, use of campus recreation center, intramurals, and outdoor trips. These data will be further applied to this end in tandem with the SRI and other ACT, Inc. data with the goal of establishing models through longitudinal tracking of performance and persistence.

Findings

Ultimately, our mission was to create a mechanism that provided opportunities for *proactive, intrusive interventions*. Information about specific intervention strategies, how the instrument data facilitated the identification of students, and the number of students who participated can be found in Table 1.

Lessons Learned

Now moving into our third year of using a student success tool to identify and provide proactive outreach to first-year students, we have learned many lessons about the implementation and ourselves:

- The timing of providing the results to students is key and directly relates to students' development and immersion in the campus community. Results must be disseminated quickly to resonate with students since the way they perceive themselves changes rapidly during the transition from high school to college.
- As multiple outreach efforts can be overwhelming to the student, a clear algorithm (identifying who will be contacted by which office, when, and how) must be collaboratively designed and understood.
- Student interventions are resource-intensive and require prioritizing groups of students. Philosophical and practical decisions regarding which students to aggressively pursue must be made. Will it be the most at-risk (most resource intensive) or a less marginal group (requiring fewer resources), and which group is the most likely to benefit from the intervention?
- We are adept at identifying and contacting those in need, but in all our efforts, we are least successful in encouraging those students to use campus resources.

Table 1

Specific Proactive Intervention Strategies Used to Meet Project Goals, Target Population, and Participants

Campus partner	Proactive intervention	Target population	Participants
Strategy 1: Identification and outreach			
The Gateway Student Success Center	Sent handwritten postcards offering students additional, focused advising	Students with low retention scores on SRI	300
Retention Alert Program (RAP)	Enrolled students in web-based program that allowed faculty to enter specific information about course performance, followed by one-on-one session with RAP advisor	Students with low retention scores on SRI	300
Multicultural Student Center	Conducted individual sessions with STAR (Successful Transition and Academic Readiness) students to go over SRI results and make appropriate referrals to campus resources	Member in STAR program	89
Native American Student Services	Made individual contact and held mentoring sessions which included referrals to appropriate campus resources	Selected Native American students using SRI composite indices and subscale scores in conjunction with best theory and practice related to facilitating academic success with this population	27
Strategy 2: Match student needs with university services			
Learning Assistance Center	Sent postcards to students advertising the services of the Learning Assistance Center	Low SRI subscale scores on Academic Discipline, Study Skills, and Academic Self Confidence	1031
Learning Assistance Center	Sent students outreach e-mail with workshop schedule and service information	Students with low scores on academic difficulty and students identified as at risk by the Gateway Student Success Center, Native American Student Services, and the Multicultural Student Center	72
Multicultural Student Center (MSC)	Sent invitations to MSC events and program every one to two weeks	Students of color with low retention scores	62

Table 1 continued p. 32

Table 1 continued

Campus partner	Proactive intervention	Target population	Participants
Strategy 2: Match student needs with university services			
Residence Life and New Student Programs	Contacted students about employment and leadership positions in their respective units	Students with high scores on one of the following SRI subscales: General Determination, Social Connection, Communication Skills, and Goal Striving	409
Residence Life and New Student Programs	Contacted students about employment and leadership positions in their respective units with specific emphasis on positive impact on first-generation students	Students with high subscale scores on General Determination, Social Connection, Communication Skills, and Goal Striving who were also first-generation students	112
Gateway Student Success Center	Sent regular e-mails announcing important deadlines, services, and events	Students with low retention scores on SRI	359
Strategy 3: Embed the SRI in our first-year seminars			
FYE 101	Developed lesson plans which used subscale scores for student reflection and decision making.	All students enrolled in FYE 101	920
EPS 101	Developed lesson plans which used subscale scores for student reflection and decision making.	All students enrolled in EPS 101	303
EPS 101	Conducted one-on-one sessions with students to review the entire SRI report and develop action plans	All students enrolled in EPS 101	303

Conclusions

Critical Elements

Our use of two different commercially prepared student success tools has facilitated our understanding of the essential ingredients for a successful implementation on our campus. First, the development, conversations, and agreement about our "understandings" have been essential to success. These understandings not only frame all of our activities but also provide us with a common vision.

Second, it is necessary to have a supportive administrative team who understands that the institutional implementation of any project requiring involvement across offices and programs is not a "retention band aid," but something that takes time, development, and tweaking. Our administration provided financial resources and devoted key staff to the implementation and assessment of the project.

A final critical element was limiting the creation of new programs or services just to fit the student success tool we selected. Rather, we decided, a priori, which of the instrument's scales matched our existing programs and services and how we would use the scales to identify students and provide outreach.

Implications and Recommendations

In a climate where new students are often overwhelmed with opportunities to be involved and paralyzed by the volume of choice, a collaborative approach to matching students to particular services offers benefits to other institutions. Several components of our approach are transferable:

- Move beyond only assisting students who did not perform well in high school or on entrance exams by identifying other variables known to relate to college student success. We chose a commercially available tool to facilitate this, but other mechanisms are also possible.
- Create a collaborative approach that brings together existing and parallel efforts on campus to join under a common vision.
- Tailor communications about specific services to students with particular needs. Students today expect us to use what we know about them to meet their needs just like they expect Amazon.com to recommend a book to them based on their profiles of past purchases. Rather than feel too intrusive, use all that has been gathered about students to offer them what we can best determine they might need.

References

Astin, A. W., Panos, R. J., & Creager, J. A. (1966). A program of longitudinal research in higher education. *ACE Research Report 1*(1). Washington, DC: American Council on Education.

Bar-On, R. (2004). The Bar-On Emotional Quotient Inventory (EQ-i): Rationale, description and summary of psychometric properties. In G. Geher (Ed.), *Measuring emotional intelligence: Common ground and controversy* (pp. 115-145). Hauppauge, NY: Nova Science.

Gore, P. A., Jr. (2006). Using academic self-efficacy to predict college outcomes: Two incremental validity studies. *Journal of Career Assessment, 14*, 92-115.

Le, H., Casillas, A., Robbins, S. B., & Langley, R. (2005). Motivational and skills, social, and self-management predictors of college outcomes: Constructing the Student Readiness Inventory. *Educational and Psychological Measurement, 65*(3), 482-508.

Robbins, S. B., Allen, J., Casillas, A., Peterson, C. H., & Le, H. (2006). Unraveling the differential effects of standardized achievement and psychosocial predictors of college outcomes: A prospective study. *Journal of Educational Psychology, 98*, 598-616.

Robbins, S. B., Lauver, K., Le, H., Davis, D., Langley, R., & Carlstrom, A. (2004). Do psychosocial and study skills factors predict college outcomes? A meta-analysis. *Psychological Bulletin, 130*, 261-288.

Stratil, M. (2004). *College Student Inventory.* Iowa City, IO: Noel-Levitz.

Primary contributor

Rebecca Pollard Cole
Coordinator, Freshmen Academic Programs
Associate Professor, Educational Psychology
Northern Arizona University
Box 5774
Flagstaff, Arizona 86011-5774
Phone: 928-523-8225
E-mail: Rebecca.Cole@nau.edu

Additional Contributors

Margot Saltonstall
Assessment Coordinator, Enrollment Management and Student Affairs
Northern Arizona University

Paul Gore
Associate Professor and Student Success Special Projects Coordinator
University of Utah

University of South Carolina

Institution Profile

Columbia, SC
Public, Four-Year
Early Intervention -
Diagnostic Tools

Editors' Notes

The University of South Carolina's Early Intervention Initiative (EII) is based in large part on the Pathfinder Program at Mississippi State University but also draws on research and affirmed best practices, which has been essential in securing faculty leadership and involvement. The program monitors attendance in select first-year courses, with cooperative and escalating interventions by faculty, academic advisors, and student affairs staff. The result has been better attendance, improved academic performance by targeted students, and better overall academic outcomes in participating first-year courses.

The Institution

Chartered in 1801, the University of South Carolina is located in the state capital of Columbia and offers a comprehensive range of undergraduate and graduate programs through the doctoral level. A major teaching and research institution, USC Columbia is a four-year public university enrolling slightly more than 18,000 undergraduate students, of whom approximately 3,700 were classified as first-year students in fall 2005. While 40% of undergraduate students are residential, approximately 95% of first-year students live in campus housing. Approximately 20% of undergraduates are students of color, with 14% African American, 3% Asian American, and 2% Hispanic. Women represent 54% of the undergraduate students, with men representing 46% of this population. While 88% of the overall undergraduate student population is from South Carolina, approximately 35% of first-year students are from out of state. The undergraduate population is traditional in age, with fewer than 5% of this population over the age of 25. Approximately one third of students are first-generation, with 28% of students responding that neither parent had completed a four-year college degree on the 2005 CIRP Freshman Survey, a percentage that has been similarly reported on other surveys.

Description of the Initiative

The Early Intervention Initiative (EII) is a cross-campus partnership between the Division of Student Affairs, First-Year English, and University 101, USC Columbia's internationally recognized seminar course dedicated to helping new students succeed. Developed through collaborative discussions among representatives from each of these areas in the spring of 2005 and implemented during the 2005-2006 academic year, the purpose of the EII is to intervene with first-year students who are excessively absent from class so that they can overcome obstacles that prevent them from meeting their academic responsibilities. The EII also serves to connect chronically absent students with helpful campus resources before their problems become too overwhelming to overcome.

The Early Intervention Initiative is research-based and modeled after best practices highlighted in such student success literature such as *Student Success in College* (Kuh, Kinzie Schuh, & Whitt, 2005), the 2004 ACT reports *What Works in Student Retention (*Habley & McClanahan*)* and *The Role of Academic and Non-Academic Factors in Improving College Retention* (Lutkowski, Robbins & Noeth), and the 2004 Pell Institute report *Raising the Graduation Rates of Low-Income College Students* (Muraskin & Lee). This body of scholarship emphasizes the importance of clearly marking pathways to success through articulating expectations, monitoring student progress in meeting these expectations, and intervening when students begin to demonstrate problems that could impede their success. A common theme shared by this body of research is that early warning systems play a key role in keeping students on track.

Absences serve as the "red flag" for the Early Intervention Initiative for several reasons, most importantly because of the documented link between class attendance and student retention. Higher education scholarship has not only "consistently found a significant negative correlation between absences and grades" (Richie & Hargrove, 2005, p. 396), but national data also demonstrate a relationship between first-year grades and persistence to degree completion (Gladieux & Perna, 2005). USC Columbia data also indicate a relationship between first-year students' grades and their likelihood to graduate from the university, even when incoming student characteristics are taken into account. Additionally, class absences give the instructor an objective, tangible point at which to intervene with a student and can be an early indicator that a student is experiencing serious emotional, mental, or physical health issues. It is usually an earlier indicator of progress than grades on tests or assignments and can serve as an early sign that a student is experiencing issues with academic-related skills, self-confidence, or goals—factors found to be significantly related to student retention.

The Early Intervention Initiative consists of a multi-faceted series of intentionally designed interventions targeting students enrolled in University 101 and English 101/102. The intervention focuses on these students for several reasons. First, the vast majority of first-year students at USC Columbia are enrolled in at least one, if not both, of these courses; thus this initiative can benefit virtually all first-year students. Second, the small class sizes in these courses make it more manageable to monitor attendance, a crucial element of the intervention. Finally, these programs were already guided by a student success philosophy, and the directors of these programs supported the voluntary participation of their faculty in this initiative. This philosophical congruence and structural support ensured a critical mass of instructors were onboard with the purpose of this initiative from the start.

The Early Intervention Initiative consists of four major components that build sequentially upon one another in response to a student's absences from University 101 or English 101/102.

1. *Clear and positive articulation of class attendance expectations by the course instructor.* Instructors not only include their attendance policies on their syllabi, but they also explain the benefits students gain from attending class regularly and the rationale for monitoring attendance in their course.

2. *Instructor interventions with students at their second class absence.* The purpose of these conversations is three-fold: (a) to let students know that their absences were noticed; (b) to reiterate the role of class attendance in meeting academic goals; and (c) to assess whether it would be helpful to make a referral to another campus resource, such as the counseling center or financial aid office.

3. *Excessive absence responder interventions with students at their third class absence.* Designated representatives from residence life, greek life, student disability services, multicultural student affairs, and athletics are notified when instructors refer students with three absences to the director

of retention and planning. Responders (a) make personal contact with students falling under their service areas, (b) inform students they have been made aware of the absences through their official capacity with USC's EII (FERPA allows disclosure to university officials with legitimate educational interests), (c) emphasize that they and the instructors care about the students' academic success and personal well-being, (d) explain that attending class is essential for succeeding academically at USC, (e) explore the situation with the students to see if it would be helpful to refer them to other campus resources, and (f) document the interventions with the director of retention and planning. This is a particularly significant point in the intervention process as students are on the cusp of having missed 10% of their class sessions, the mark at which they can receive a grading penalty.

4.   *Participation in class absence reflection (CAR) group at fourth class absence.* Facilitated by staff in the Counseling and Human Development Center, the Class Absence Reflection (CAR) Group gives students the opportunity to "think out loud" about their specific circumstances, academic goals, priorities, and habits in order to improve their performance at USC. Instructors can choose to delay the grading penalty for excessive absences if students attend the CAR Group and complete a series of reflection questions based on their experience.

Research Design

The Early Intervention Initiative attempts to solve the following problems related to first-year student issues:

1.   *How can we improve student adjustment from a regimented and highly supervised high school environment to a more unstructured college environment in which students receive less direct supervision?* The EII attempts to promote positive transitions through articulating the importance of regular class attendance and intervening with students who begin to get off track.

2.   *What strategies can we implement to effectively reduce the number of students missing class excessively?* Based on research by Friedman, Rodriguez, and McComb (2001), the EII attempts to demonstrate to students that attendance does impact their grades and that professors do notice and care when they are in class.

3.   *How can we get students experiencing serious transition or health issues to connect with campus resources before their problems become too overwhelming to overcome?* Given that many students experience depression and suicidal ideation (American College Health Association, 2005), the EII attempts to create a clear channel by which faculty members can appropriately refer students experiencing mental health issues.

4.   *How can we identify those issues that are most strongly related to chronic absenteeism for first-year students?* The EII attempts to assess faculty and student perceptions related to chronic absenteeism in order to implement proactive strategies that get to the core of the issue.

5.   *How can the University demonstrate that it cares about student success on an individual level?* The EII attempts to demonstrate to students that despite USC's size, it is an institution at which they cannot be anonymous and at which they cannot easily fall through the cracks.

6.   *How can we further develop collaborative partnerships between student affairs and academic affairs?* The EII attempts to promote cross-campus dialogue about student success and to create structures that enhance communication and support in addressing student issues.

Although this initiative is still in its infancy, several means of assessment have been developed to examine the impact of the Early Intervention Initiative, including:

1.   *End of the semester progress reports.* Completed by instructors for each student referred to the director of retention and planning for three or more absences, the progress reports collect data on total absences, reasons for absences, types of interventions students received, perceived impact of the intervention, and class grade. During fall 2005, one third ($n = 47$) of U101 instructors

referred 101 students with three or more absences to the director of retention and planning. End of semester progress reports were submitted for 92 of these students.

2. *End of semester instructor evaluations.* Instructors who referred students for three or more absences complete an evaluation asking for their feedback on the effectiveness of the EII. During fall 2005, 60% (*n* = 28) of referring instructors completed evaluations.

3. *Class absence reflection group pre- and postsurveys.* Students attending the CAR Group complete a pre-workshop survey assessing issues related to absenteeism as well as a post-workshop survey assessing the attainment of outcomes. During fall 2005, 30 students attended a CAR Group workshop (10% of these had also been referred for three or more absences).

Findings

Data collected through the above assessments indicate that the Early Intervention Initiative has begun to successfully address several issues related to first-year student success.

Improving Student Adjustment

According to one instructor, the EII has helped "to save some kids who can do the work, but have other issues such as time management, health, etc." One way it has enhanced student transitions is through providing a framework for instructors to "talk about attendance more and from a positive stance rather than a punitive stance."

Reducing Excessive Absences

Seventy-two percent of referring instructors noted that the EII made a positive difference in their students' class attendance patterns, with 50% of the students referred accumulating no more than four absences during the course of the semester. Students also noted that as a result of attending the CAR group session they had a better understanding of issues preventing them from getting to class (88%) and had a plan that would help them attend class more regularly (80%).

Routing Students to Resources

Instructors officially referred 122 students to campus resources through the EII. Approximately 60% of the students attending the CAR group indicated a plan to use campus services, including individual counseling and tutoring.

Identifying Issues Related to Absenteeism

When asked to rate the reasons contributing to their absenteeism, CAR group participants identified (a) being out too late, partying, or alcohol/drug use (40%); (b) feeling the class was not worthwhile (30%); and (c) feeling ill or in over their heads (20%).

Demonstrating a Caring Environment

One instructor noted, "My students said that the intervention really drove some issues home, made them feel less like a number, and provided the push they so desperately needed."

Developing Collaborative Partnerships

Ninety-three percent of referring instructors responded that they would recommend the EII to other instructors because they "appreciated having a sense there was a network of resources available to help them address some serious issues."

Conclusions

The considerable time dedicated to collaborative dialogue during the development of the EII helped to minimize the challenges and barriers in implementing the initiative. However, we did learn several lessons from our experience. First, some instructors were reluctant to participate in the EII because they felt they were "turning students in." We have responded by clearly emphasizing the positive and supportive nature of the initiative and by changing our language from "reporting" an excessively absent student to "referring" a student to resources. Second, this is a time-intensive initiative for instructors and responders, and we have attempted to streamline the referral and tracking processes to make the process more user-friendly. Finally, it may have been helpful to designate experimental and control groups during the first year of implementation in order to more effectively measure the impact of the intervention. However, the student success literature and national data present such powerful support for early interventions that it seemed most ethical to make this initiative available to all instructors.

Several critical elements had to be in place to promote the success of the initiative. First and foremost, it required the identification of the key campus players, the development of collaborative partnerships between these educators and professionals, and the involvement of all parties in the development and implementation of the model. Another critical element was the extensive research conducted to understand the issues and intentionally develop the initiative. A third critical element was the identification of a key person to coordinate the logistics related to the development, implementation, and evaluation of the initiative. A final critical element was the development of an assessment plan to evaluate the success and effectiveness of the initiative.

The Early Intervention Initiative poses many implications for educational practice with first-year students. Millennial students are accustomed to (and they and their parents expect) frequent feedback about their progress, and this initiative is one way to enhance the transition of this generation of students to the college environment. It also has implications for student success, especially as institutions of higher education are facing mounting demands to demonstrate effectiveness and efficiency in graduating students. Additionally, since the research exists to support the critical role of class attendance and early interventions in promoting student success, a final implication relates to institutions' ethical responsibilities to act upon this knowledge.

Authors' Note

We would like to especially recognize Mississippi State University's Pathfinder's program as a primary model in the development of the Early Intervention Initiative.

References

American College Health Association. (2005). *National College Health Assessment: Reference group data report fall 2004*. Baltimore, MD: Author. Retrieved December 18, 2007 from http://wwwacha-ncha.org/pubs_rpts. html

Friedman, P., Rodriguez, F., & McComb, J. (2001). Why students do and do not attend classes. *College Teaching, 49*(4), 124-133.

Gladieux, L., & Perna, L. (2005). Borrowers who drop out: A neglected aspect of the college student load trend. Washington, DC: The National Center for Public Policy and Higher Education.

Habley, W. R., & McClanahan, R. (2004). *What works in student retention – four year public institutions*. Iowa City: ACT, Inc.

Kuh, G. D., Kinzie, J., Schuh, J. H., & Whitt, E. J. (2005). *Student success in college*. San Francisco: Jossey-Bass.

Lotkowski, V. A., Robbins, S. B., & Noeth, R. J. (2004). *The role of academic and non-academic factors in improving college student retention.* Iowa City: ACT, Inc.

Muraskin, L. & Lee, J. (2004). *Raising the graduation rates of low-income college students.* Washington, DC: The Pell Institute.

Richie, S. D. & Hargrove, D. S. (2005). An analysis of the effectiveness of telephone intervention in reducing absences and improving grades of college freshmen. *Journal of College Student Retention, 6*(4), 395-412.

Primary Contributor

Chrissy Coley
Assistant Vice Provost, Student Success Initiatives

Additional Contributor

Russell Haber
Director, Counseling and Human Development Center
University of South Carolina
James F. Byrnes Building
Columbia, SC 29208
Phone: 803-777-5223
E-mail: rhaber@sc.edu

Section 3
First-Year Advising

Bridgewater State College

Institution Profile

*Bridgewater, MA
Public, Four-Year
First-Year Advising*

Editors' Notes

The Haughey First Year Program, implemented in the spring of 1999, was developed in response to a growing frustration among academic advisors that even though much time and energy was spent seeing students, the contacts were largely logistical in nature (related to registration procedures) and not conducive to deeper levels of learning and development. The revision to five mandatory contacts during the first semester is not unique to effective advising programs, but the strategic nature of the contacts is notable. The outcomes-based development of content and intentional delivery schedule reveals a curricular approach to academic advising that is both pedagogically and logistically sound. This is an example of a truly replicable advising curriculum.

The Institution

Bridgewater State College is the largest state college in the Massachusetts public higher education system and is the fifth largest campus overall in the system, which comprises 15 community colleges, nine state colleges, and a university with five campuses.

The undergraduate FTE was 6,506 in fall 2004 and 6,608 in fall 2005, with approximately 1,400 first-year students. Undergraduate enrollment in fall 2005 was 40% male and 60% female, and students of color comprised 7% of the 2005 first-year class. Among students of color, students who identify as African American comprised the largest group, followed in succession by Hispanic, Asian, and Native American. International students comprised 1% of total undergraduate enrollment. Among students who apply for financial aid, 60% reported that at least one parent attended college. Those who are 25 or older are 18% of college enrollment. While demand for on-campus housing is great (85-90% of applicants request housing), only 720 first- year students can be accommodated. In all, two thirds of Bridgewater students are commuters.

The Description of Initiative

The Haughey First Year Program was initiated in the spring semester of 1999. The program delivers a comprehensive advising curriculum through a minimum of five mandatory advising contacts. The advising curriculum is continually reviewed and enhanced through collaborative work of faculty advisors, professional staff, and graduate assistants. Two guiding questions help define the content of the advising program:

- What do beginning first-year students need to know and be able to do to successfully manage their academic careers?
- At what point in the period of time from orientation through the first college semester are specific skills and knowledge most needed?

Students participate in four required group-advising sessions and at least one individual advising session to gain access to registration for the second college semester. See Appendix for an outline of the advising curriclum.

Students with significant academic risk are identified for placement in courses with attached learning assistance. Scores from mandatory entry assessment of reading, writing, and mathematics are cross-referenced with high school GPA and SAT scores and intended major. Students who place in pre-college writing and/or present a reading score below criterion are required to enroll in sections of college-level writing I that include participation in a book club, weekly individual work with an undergraduate writing fellow, a weekly small-group study session, contact with a peer advisor, and additional individual advising contact with the assigned academic advisor. Students with an intended major that requires calculus, who present entry assessment scores considerably below what is required for placement in college-level math, are required to complete a noncredit pre-college math course and participate in a weekly small group study session facilitated by an undergraduate math coach (students majoring in education and either mathematics or science). Individuals who present scores that are closer to the cut score for college-level math placement are required to complete pre-calculus and participate in a weekly study session, also facilitated by an undergraduate math coach.

Administration of the Initiative.

The first-year program serves all beginning students with fewer than 12 earned college credits (exclusive of advanced placement credits). Serving approximately 1,400 students necessitates a highly collaborative approach and involves numerous offices and personnel from across divisions. For example, delivery of orientation placement testing, advising, and special placements requires the cooperation of the Academic Achievement Center, Office of Student Affairs, the Office of Admissions, and the Registrar's Office. The collaboration required to deliver advising and courses with attached learning assistance involves an even greater number of people.

The first-year advising program strives to maintain at least 1.50 FTE faculty involvement, and makes use of five graduate assistants, three part-time professional advisors, one full-time staff advisor, an assistant director of the Academic Achievement Center, and five or more undergraduate peer advisors. Courses targeted for special placement of students at-risk involve 15 or more faculty instructors; four faculty directors of learning assistance services; six graduate assistants; 36 volunteer book club facilitators drawn from the ranks of campus faculty, staff, and administrators; as many volunteer undergraduate student co-facilitators as can be recruited; 10 undergraduate writing fellows; and seven undergraduate math coaches.

Research Design

The impetus for development of the Haughey First Year Program was frustration among faculty and staff advisors. Advisors expressed concern that the lack of sufficient contact with their advisees (only during drop/add and pre-registration) resulted in students' developmental challenges not being systematically addressed.

A number of quantitative measures of program effectiveness routinely collected and used in defining and refining program delivery include:

- First- and second-year persistence rates
- First-semester academic standing (percentage in good standing, on academic probation, or academically dismissed)
- Second-semester academic standing
- Second- and third-year persistence

- Persistence and academic standing among students in targeted mathematics and writing courses after the first college semester and beyond
- Outcomes among students who complete math and writing courses with attached learning assistance compared to outcomes observed among all first-year students
- Persistence and academic standing of special populations (e.g., special admits, students with disabilities, students of color)
- Six-year graduation rate
- Attainment of Dean's List in first college semester

Qualitative assessment is routinely conducted through advising sessions when students are asked to complete questionnaires about session content and are provided the opportunity to write questions that can be answered via individual e-mail contact. Students are also encouraged to respond to an online survey about academic advising that is available to all students each semester after pre-registration. Quantitative trends over the course of the program (1999 to present), including information gleaned from surveys and observation of program efforts, informs both the content and delivery of the advising program in subsequent semesters.

Findings

In the early years of the Haughey First Year Program, college admission standards were raised from a minimum high school GPA of 2.70/ 4.0 (1998 and 1999) to a minimum 2.90/ 4.0 (2000) and, in 2001, to the current requirement of 3.00 on 16 college preparation units. With the admission standard as a filter through which outcomes can be viewed, some encouraging trends emerge. Since the Haughey Program has come into full effect, persistence of all students at Bridgewater State College has increased, rising from 69% for the fall 1999 entering class to 78% for the fall 2003 entering class. For special admits, persistence (defined as percentage of students who complete their third term) has increased from 59% to 78%. For students with documented disabilities, persistence increased from 75% to 84% over the same time period. Similar increases have been observed for students of color (64% to 77%) and at-risk students of color (i.e., special admits; 57% to 73%). Such improvements suggest that the series of mandatory contacts, array of programs, and systematic delivery of academic support services have had a marked impact on the transition success of Bridgewater students.

The campus is equally interested in whether a strong emphasis on the transition to college for first-year students positions them for success and persistence into and beyond the third college year. Third-year persistence for the class entering in 1998 was 83% and has risen to 87% for the 2002 class.

Outcomes specific to Writing I, through which developmental reading and writing needs are addressed, reveal that students in targeted sections pass the course at nearly the same rate as students who earn placement in regular Writing I. For students placed in targeted sections of pre-calculus, preliminary outcomes are encouraging. Students enrolled in fall 2005 and spring 2006 presented D/F/W/IN rates of 35% and 23%, compared to rates of 50% and 53% among regular sections where no systematic learning assistance was delivered.

Finally, first-semester Dean's List attainment (3.30 or higher GPA on 12 college credits) provides an interesting indicator of enhancements in students' achievement since the time first-year program changes were implemented. For the class of 2000, the rate of Dean's List attainment in the first college semester was 14%. While admission standards have remained the same, the percentage of first-year students earning Dean's List distinction has since increased steadily (14% in 2002, 16% in 2003, 17% in both 2004 and 2005), reaching a high of 22% in the fall of 2006. The kind of support imbedded in targeted courses continues to evolve, informed by assessment of students' learning outcomes.

Conclusions

Success of the Haughey First Year Program is contingent upon a great deal of sustained and widespread collaboration. An important lesson learned is the wisdom of initiating program components incrementally. It is through the dissemination and celebration of observed outcomes that trust, support, and enthusiasm for new approaches are built. In the case of the Haughey First Year Program, advising was the primary focus.

Another learned lesson relates to the critical importance of collaborating widely, fostering necessary coordination among all key offices and administrative units, and maintaining a high level of faculty involvement. For example, maintenance of target course initiatives hinges upon ongoing cooperation among the faculty and staff of the first-year program, the Registrar's Office, department chairs, deans, and faculty of targeted courses through which the developmental writing, reading, and mathematics needs of students are addressed. Fostering such collaboration requires attention to issues of trust, maintenance of rigorous academic standards, a universal commitment to the concept of mandatory student involvement, and attention to the continuing need for communication among all who work with students being served through the initiatives.

A final important lesson is that earnestly assessing and sharing student learning outcomes is imperative. Sharing student learning outcomes fosters a culture of data-driven collaboration. The data identifies student needs, which can inform planning of systematic efforts to assist students who are not thriving on campus.

Administrator support is a critical element in the planning and facilitation of training sessions and meetings among all who participate in advising or delivery of targeted courses. This model necessitates sharing information about students among involved faculty, staff, peer educators, and administrators. The administrators are well-positioned to create and sustain the structures necessary for these initiatives.

Another critical element of the model in place at Bridgewater State College is the linking of first-year advising and focused delivery of learning assistance. This approach, which provides a means of addressing transition concerns of individual students, is contingent upon a high degree of faculty commitment and involvement in instruction, advising, and delivery of focused learning assistance. Faculty involvement can be fostered by offering course releases and/or extra compensation during the academic year and through the summer orientation season.

The model in place at Bridgewater State College addresses assumptions commonly made about what students should know about the college experience through an advising program that systematically teaches such skills and knowledge. Further, the model identifies students' needs for developmental instruction and learning assistance via indicators like SAT scores and entry assessment of mathematics, reading, and writing rather than demographic characteristics like race. Finally, the model increases campus-wide understanding of the challenges faced by beginning first-year students often for people who typically have limited student contact.

Advice to anyone interested in adapting the Bridgewater model for their own campus centers on the importance of starting from a perspective of what can be done to better support the successful transition of all first-year students (e.g., mandatory group advising with a standard curriculum), and then systematically assessing institutional outcome data to determine populations of students who can benefit from additional focused attention (e.g., courses with attached learning assistance and/or additional advising attention). The journey at Bridgewater State College has brought about tremendous change and continues to amaze all who are involved by continually revealing more that can be done to support our students' college experience. A focused beginning and strategic, incremental program additions have contributed to a campus culture and results we celebrate.

Primary Contributor

Peggy J. Smith
Director, Academic Achievement Center
Bridgewater State College
Bridgewater, MA 02325
Phone: 508-531-1214
E-mail: p1smith@bridgew.edu

Appendix
First-Year Advising Components

Advising Session	When	Goal	Objectives	Staffing
Advising 101	Orientation	Course schedule planning and knowledge to support successful management of academic career	College polices and processes; general education requirements, majors requirements, prerequisite course schedule bulletin, catalog, and other tools of course selection	Faculty advisor, academic counselor, orientation leaders
Advising 102	Orientation	Development of an appropriate first-semester course schedule	Registration informed by placement testing, general education requirements, major requirements	Faculty advisor, academic counselor, orientation leaders
Individual advising for students in special placement	Weeks 1-16 of first semester	Attention to the adjustment and achievement of at-risk students	Course-by-course assessment, college adjustment	Faculty advisor
Large group	Weeks 3-4 of first semester	Process of academic advising, academic planning, and academic survival skills	Advising and registration process, campus resources, academic standards and GPA calculation, current academic functioning	Faculty advisor, staff member, academic counselor, peer advisor
Small group (by major)	Weeks 7-9 of first semester	Major and general education requirements and planning for next semester	Prerequisites in current schedule, general education and major requirements, use of course schedule and catalog	Faculty advisor, academic counselor, peer advisor
Individual	Weeks 8-10 of first semester	Attention to the experience of individual student	Course-by-course assessment, college adjustment, life and career goals, curriculum of upcoming semester	Faculty advisor, peer advisor

Appendix continued p. 49

Appendix continued

Advising Session	When	Goal	Objectives	Staffing
Additional undeclared advising	Weeks 4-7 of first semester	Assist students to make an informed declaration of major	Assess progress in ongoing stages of decision making, determine next steps	Faculty advisor
Group academic probation advising	Weeks 3-4 of second semester	Assist students in achieving good academic standing	Assess reasons for academic probation, express academic concerns and semester goals, graduation requirements and academic standards, GPA calculation, campus resources	Staff member, academic counselor, peer advisor
Individual academic probation advising	Weeks 4-16 of second semester	Assist students in achieving good academic standing	Assessment of performance in courses, referral to appropriate learning assistance and other support services	Faculty advisor
Additional undeclared advising	Weeks 1-16 of each semester	Assist those undeclared students beyond their first semester to make an informed declaration of major	Assess progress in ongoing stages of decision making, determine next steps	Faculty advisor

Indiana Wesleyan University

Institution Profile

Marion, IN
Private, Four-Year
First-Year Advising

Editors' Notes

The first year of college is a time of significant transition for all students, but it can be particularly challenging for those who have not yet determined an academic focus. "Pre-declared" students at Indiana Wesleyan University are given the opportunity to engage in purposeful exploration of disciplinary choices through a series of instructional and developmental activities designed to integrate both personal self-reflection and institutional intervention through the first-year seminar and academic advising.

The Institution

Indiana Wesleyan University (IWU) is a comprehensive, private university with its main campus in Marion, Indiana. IWU's mission is to produce students prepared and committed to engagement in world changing endeavors. An evangelical Christian commitment permeates the university's programming and culture and guides an institutional focus on encouraging students to pursue their life purpose. IWU enrolls almost 9,000 full-time undergraduate students and 5,000 graduate students. The undergraduate population is 61.5% female and 38.5% male. Of those enrolled in traditional undergraduate programs, 96.8% are age 24 and under. Students of color include African American (.83%), Hispanic (.97%), Asian American (.37%), and Native American (.23%). Retention rates at IWU continue to climb as the first-year experience program becomes more firmly integrated into the campus culture through collaborative efforts of the College of Arts and Sciences, student development, residence life, student support services, and the Center for Life Calling and Leadership. With the advent of increased emphases on first-year programming, IWU retention rates have risen from 65% in 1996 to 83% in 2006, and five-year graduation rates have risen 30% since 1991, to 66%.

Description of the Initiative

According to data from the 2006 Cooperative Institutional Research Program (CIRP) Freshmen Survey, students arriving at IWU have decided to attend college for rather typical reasons (e.g., because my parents wanted me to go to college, to get a better job, to get training for a specific career). Interestingly, when these students came to campus for summer registration, approximately 16% of them reported that they were undecided in regard to a preferred college major. On the CIRP, however, only 5.8% of these same first-year students indicated they were undecided. The discrepancy between summer notations and the CIRP data seem to reflect the availability of a list of potential majors instead of an open-ended question (e.g., "What is your intended major?"). Regardless, 16% of the first-year students remained officially undeclared via information from our Records Office. These data seemingly point to three things that we already know about college students: (a) the college years are a time of growth and change, (b) determinations regarding major areas of study and future professions continue to emerge and be refined during the college experience, and (c) the college years can be a time when students are provided with intentional experiences that assist them in clarifying and pursuing a purpose for their life. It is this third dynamic that characterizes IWU's student success strategy.

As part of an ongoing process of self-study in relation to the various components of the IWU first-year experience, we began to investigate the role of life purpose in the lives and decision-making processes of first-year students. On our campus, approximately 16% of first-year students who come to summer registration have not identified a major and are referred to as "pre-declared." IWU's overriding emphasis on life calling and purpose diffuses subtle pressure that first-year students had earlier reported. They become more open to the exploration and declaration of a major in the search for a career and life purpose. Our goal is to facilitate decision making in an individualized manner that appreciates and acknowledges the needs of the student.

The needs and interests of first-year students who have not declared a major are addressed from three perspectives: (a) realignment of the first-year seminar to reflect an added emphasis on the issues of life calling and purpose, (b) use of the Center for Life Calling and Leadership in advising pre-declared students to take a special course offering that integrates the issue of life calling, and (c) integration of these components in the context of student advising.

Realignment of the First-Year Seminar

A foundational component of the first-year experience is the seminar "Becoming World Changers" that involves all first-year students. The first-year experience is strongly aligned with the concept of life purpose (Figure 1). As one of the most important parts of the first-year experience, the first-year seminar has been realigned to reflect this emphasis. We define life purpose as a confidence in an overriding purpose for your life and living your life in congruence with that purpose.

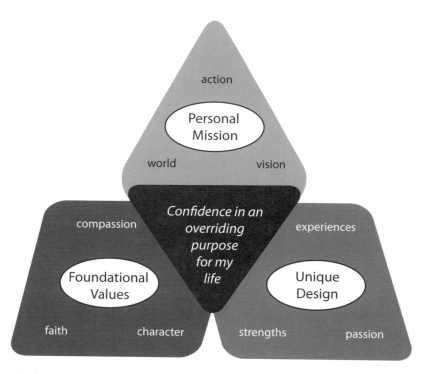

Figure 1. The Life Purpose Model.

As part of the content for this course, students examine critical perspectives related to life purpose, including:

- Understanding and articulating their life dreams
- Identifying heroes and world changers
- Clarifying the characteristics and qualities of noble causes
- Identifying and valuing their own unique gifts and talents
- Pursuing their life calling—a purpose-based approach to life experience

Additionally, as students participate in the first-year seminar, they are asked to process and complete assignments that assist in focusing their understanding and personalization of life purpose. These include:

- Development of an "I Have A Dream" essay that articulates their views of a desirable vision for the future of the culture and the planet
- Writing a "Letter Home" in which they share their reasons for pursuing a college education with another person of their choosing
- Formulation of a "Personal Mission Statement" (that will ultimately be returned to them for review and reflection during their final year of college)

Use of the Center for Life Calling and Leadership

A second and critical component of this process involves the services and resources of The Center for Life Calling and Leadership (CLCL). The CLCL provides a variety of assessment and advising services that assist students in clarifying their own gifts, strengths, and talents as they relate to the big picture of a life purpose. The Center also facilitates a course that systematically guides students on an exploration of the three identified components of life purpose as it is conceptualized at IWU: unique strengths, foundational values, and personal mission. Additionally, life coaches from the Center also serve as faculty for the "Introduction to Life Calling" course. Students who enter the university in a pre-declared status are strongly encouraged to take this course in their first semester on campus. The activities, assessments, and assignments that are integral to this course also reflect a focus on assisting students as they integrate themselves into the flow of college life. This course has a strong focus on the following areas of concern:

- Developing a sense of purpose and calling as a basis for making life decisions
- Selecting and scheduling courses
- Establishing and evaluating academic goals
- Understanding and navigating university academic policies and procedures
- Exploring academic majors and related careers
- Declaring a major
- Connecting with additional university programs and resources

Academic Advising

Finally, as a means for integrating life purpose, course content, and decision making into the lives of students who are pre-declared, academic advising is administered through life coaches from the CLCL (who also serve as the faculty for the "Introduction to Life Calling" course). In this way, pre-declared students build a relationship with their advisors (i.e., life coaches) on an individual basis and within the context of the classroom. These relationships, in concert with course content and other services and supports offered on campus provide these students with a platform for processing decisions about their transition into college, academic major, and life purpose.

Research Design

In cooperation with researchers from Indiana University, the Indiana Project on Academic Success (IPAS), and the Lumina Foundation, a research project was undertaken to examine derived differences in the lives of pre-declared students. Structured by Ed St. John (now at the University of Michigan), this study also explored the possible impact on retention and persistence, as they explored the issue of life purpose through coursework and advising experiences. This study involved a four-year cohort study (n = 1,748), including the collection and analysis of qualitative and quantitative data. Three different regression analyses were conducted to examine the impact of the course "Introduction to Life Calling" (as well as other complementary supports).

Findings

The results of the IPAS study (Gross, Millard, Pattengale & Reynolds, 2006) indicate that the Life Calling course and auxiliary program supports helped participants to be:

- Almost six times more likely to persist to the next year than students who did not take part in the program during the 2000-2001 academic year
- Almost three times more likely to persist to the next year than students who did not take the course during the 2001-2002 academic year
- Six times more likely to have earned a degree at the end of four years than those who did not take the class and received auxiliary program supports
- Seventeen times more likely to remain enrolled than withdraw after four years if they had not completed their degree (in comparison with those who did not take the class)

Conclusions

This initiative has reinforced several key practices in relation to the design and implementation of first-year initiatives on our campus:

- It is critically important to acknowledge and address the concerns of first-year students in relation to persisting issues of their lives including their global purpose in life.
- The needs of first-year students can be best addressed in a comprehensive and coordinated fashion, incorporating the expertise and resources of the various components of campus life (e.g., classroom experiences, support services, advising).
- Discussions and explorations of life purpose do have a significant and dramatic impact on the retention and persistence of first-year students, especially those who enter as, or become, undeclared.
- Having chosen a major was significant to students' persistence. Therefore, this suggests that choosing a major and taking the "Introduction to Life Calling" class (and auxiliary supports) were both significantly related to persistence at IWU.
- Although the reported data were derived from a longitudinal study, additional data collection and analysis will be undertaken as a means of providing further examination of the above described hypotheses and findings regarding the role of purpose in the lives of undeclared students.

Reference

Gross, J., Millard, B., Pattengale, J., & Reynolds, P., (2006). *Discovering life purpose: Retention success in a leadership course at Indiana Wesleyan University.* Bloomington: Indiana Project on Academic Success.

Primary contributor

J. Bradley Garner
Associate Dean for Student Success
College of Arts and Sciences
Indiana Wesleyan University
4201 South Washington Street
Marion, IN 46953
Phone: 765-677-2452
E-mail: brad.garner@indwes.edu

Additional Contributors

Bill Millard
Executive Director, Center for Life Calling and Leadership
Indiana Wesleyan University

Jerry Pattengale
Assistant Vice President for Scholarship and Grants
Indiana Wesleyan University

Section 4
"Linked" Learning Communities

Slippery Rock University

Institution Profile

Slippery Rock, PA
Public, Four-Year
"Linked" Learning
Communities

Editors' Notes

The comprehensive program of linked learning communities and the first-year seminar, as well as the consistent approach to professional development, represents an intentional effort at Slippery Rock University to encourage meaningful connections at all levels of engagement. Members of the faculty, student affairs staff, and peer leaders work together to plan, implement, and assess the impact of the series of courses and activities on academic success, persistence, and integration to the institution.

The Institution

Slippery Rock University (SRU) is one of the 14 State System of Higher Education institutions in the Commonwealth of Pennsylvania. Located in rural western Pennsylvania, SRU is a public comprehensive institution with an undergraduate and graduate enrollment of about 8,105 students. About 1,500 first-time, full-time first-year students enter the university each fall. Annual first-year student survey results show that first-generation students continue to comprise the majority of the institution's new students (63%). Additionally, about 90% of SRU's students are receiving financial aid. Institutional research shows that average combined SAT scores have ranged from 945 to 1001 over the last five years, and about 35% of incoming first-year students enroll in at least one developmental course. Finally, most first-year students come from 15 counties in western Pennsylvania, many representing rural communities. Undergraduate student demographic information show that women make up a larger percentage of the undergraduate population (54%). Most students (90%) are traditional-age (18-24), and about 5% of the population are students of color (primarily African American and Hispanic). First-year students are required to live on campus, and the total on-campus population is about 2,800.

Description of the Initiative

In response to Slippery Rock University's steady decline in enrollment, strategic recruitment and persistence efforts became the top priority in 1999. With the goal of creating a campus attitude and climate consistently and intentionally focused on meeting student needs and success, high expectations were set for students, staff, faculty, and administration to assume leadership roles, work collaboratively, and assess and account for the improvement and continuation of first-year programming efforts. Although faculty within the Enrollment Services Division, along with partnerships with student affairs constituents, provided the initial First Year Studies (FYRST) programming services—specifically the first-year seminar. Faculty and administration across all disciplines now participate and have gradually taken ownership of university services for our first-year students.

In fall 2000, SRU initiated the use of a linked Learning Community Cluster (LCC) and first-year seminar effort as a key ingredient in enhancing the first-year learning and success. Research had found that first-year orientation seminars and learning community cluster programs were effective programming efforts for responding to the academic and social/personal needs of first-year students. The goals of the LCC/FYRST seminar initiative were to increase student persistence, academic performance, and academic and social integration with the institution. The student participants for the LCC/FYRST seminar initiative were first time, full-time students entering the University. The LCC/FYRST seminars consist of a small group of students sharing enrollment in several classes, a liberal studies/major program class, college writing, and the FYRST seminar. The LCC initiative has grown from 27 LCCs in 2000 to 51 LCCs in 2006. The characteristics of the program to improve student learning and success include its intentionality, the integration of efforts among personnel in all divisions of the institution, the planned interventions with students to promote achievement and success, and information-driven decision making to assess the initiative.

Faculty members serving as instructors for the course are thoughtfully solicited and selected. They attend a two-day professional development workshop, communicate through e-mail and Blackboard discussions throughout the fall, and have constant access to a wealth of supportive instructional and resource materials on a FYRST seminar Blackboard resource web site. Professional staff from the divisions of Student Life and Enrollment Services attend the training workshop and share resource materials as well.

Beginning in 2003, FYRST seminar faculty had the opportunity to use a dynamic e-learning tool as a means of increasing communication among faculty and first-year students. Faculty members were initially introduced to Blackboard, a course management system, at the professional development workshop. Through Blackboard, the FYRST seminar resource site created hosting information to develop and prepare faculty to teach the course. The resource site provided samples of course materials, resources, and activities organized by FYRST seminar topics (e.g., time management, advisement, active learning styles, diversity, relationships, study skills, wellness). Additionally, the resource site is a communication tool that assists faculty in sharing ideas with each other on what does and does not work. Blackboard was also used for a second tier of services by our faculty with a focus specifically on their respective FYRST seminar. Faculty received course shells for their individual FYRST seminar section, enabling them to post their own course materials, announcements, assignments, and grades for their students, as well as enhance communication with their students through discussion boards and e-mail.

Literature from the past four decades suggests that students can have a significant and positive impact on other students. Gardner (2001) strongly advocated peer leader programs as a means for leveraging "...an institution's chances of influencing student behaviors and attitudes in those directions in which it would like to see students move, particularly in those ways that might be consistent with the institutional mission" (p. vii). Consequently, a peer leadership component was integrated into the FYRST seminar course in 2004. Intentionally designed to further provide support, clarity, and student-centered focus for our faculty, the purpose of our FYRST Peer Leader program was two-fold: (a) peer leaders impacted first-year students positively, serving as role models, offering suggestions, providing support and encouragement, promoting self-responsibility and self-direction and (b) peer leaders, themselves, gained invaluable learning experiences by engaging in meaningful work, developing important leadership skills, learning to take responsibility, increasing contact with faculty members, and gaining a sense of self-worth.

Based on Hunter and Heath's (2001) identified elements of effective peer leading, our peer leader program—from development to implementation—was designed with a team-based, multi-level, and assessment-driven approach. All FYRST seminar faculty were provided the opportunity to partner with an upper-level undergraduate student for planning, development, and instruction of their seminar. Although program coordinators were able to provide a trained peer leader to faculty members upon request, FYRST seminar faculty were strongly encouraged to self-identify an upper-level student to serve as their peer leader—typically a student from their previous FYRST seminar course and/or an advisee within their major. Once FYRST faculty and peer leader matches were made, peer leaders participated in continual, required training and supervision. Centering on the guiding principle of true partnerships, FYRST faculty and peer leaders were provided scheduled meeting and planning opportunities not only during the FYRST faculty and peer leader professional development workshops but also during weekly throughout the entire semester of their FYRST seminar. Additionally, peer leaders met weekly as a large group with program coordinators to share ideas, plan FYRST seminar/university-wide activities, receive further training and supervision, and for team-building experiences. As recommended by Barefoot and Gardner (1993), compensation for peer leaders included monetary payment and institutional service recognition on cocurricular transcripts.

Research Design

Several types of data sources were used as assessment indicators for the program since its implementation in 2000. Quantitative and qualitative assessments on academic and social integration factors, perceived student learning outcomes, and retention tracking were undertaken. Careful attention was given to controlling the independent variable, the FYRST seminar course. Specifically, survey assessments developed by our institution were used. These instruments evaluated the FYRST Seminar Resource site and the Peer Leading Program—perceptions of students, peer leaders, and faculty. They continue to be used annually for continuous program planning and improvement. Open-ended commentary was collected from LCC/FYRST seminar faculty and students at the end of the first semester of the program as well. In addition, institutional data regarding first- to second-year persistence and five-year and six-year graduation rates were used to determine the course's influence on retention and persistence to graduation.

Finally, two national benchmarking instruments are used by the institution: The National Survey of Student Engagement and the First-Year Initiative (FYI). These instruments helped us compare the effectiveness of our programs with those of peer institutions.

Findings

In the first two years, with a 51% and 70% first-year seminar student enrollment rate respectively, we found that academic and social integration were enhanced as a result of participating in the LCC/FYRST seminar initiative. For each of the two years, students enrolled in the cluster had statistically significant greater scores on four of the five integration scales: (a) peer group interactions, (b) interactions with faculty outside of the classroom, (c) academic and intellectual development, and (d) institutional and goal commitment. Additionally, students who participated in the LCC/FYRST seminar used a significantly greater number of campus services than students not enrolled in the program. Throughout the next several years and into the program's 2006 enrollment, student involvement and participation rates increased and/or continued at the same elevated levels.

Institutional Research Data

Similarly, institutional student tracking research found that in the first two years of the program (2000-02), students who participated in the LCC/FYRST seminar persisted to their second year at a higher rate than non-participants. First- to second-year retention increased 8% for students overall, with notable improvement for at-risk students (15%) and students of color (7%). Accordingly, SRU received a national award for excellence in retention on the basis of this program in

2003. Institutional student tracking through the program's entirety and up to year 2006 reveal an overall first-to-second year retention increase of 11% since 1995, with notable improvement for at-risk students (12%), African American students (20%), and Hispanic students (31%). In review of graduation rates, six-year rates increased from 47% to 52% and five-year graduation rates from 43% (1995 cohort) to a current status of 47% (1999 cohort).

Two additional results of the program—although not found to be statistically significant—are to be noted as they do bear educational significance: (a) LCC/FYRST seminar students consistently earn more credits by the end of their first academic year than non-participants, and (b) LCC/FYRST seminar students earn higher grade point averages. Since 2001, the first-year cohort's average grade point has risen from 2.75 to 2.90.

Firs-Year Initiative Data

In the last four years of the program, the institution used the First-Year Initiative Seminar Assessment to understand SRU's student perceptions of the FYRST seminar course. The focus of the FYI assessment is on perceived student learning outcomes created by the first-year course. The analysis of responses for the other participating schools provides comparative perspectives and benchmarks on perceptions of students in similar first courses and seminars. Students participating in the FYRST seminar in fall 2005 had statistically significant higher means on all 15 student learning outcomes than students at six benchmark institutions. Learning outcomes are defined as follows:

- Course improved study strategies
- Course improved academic/cognitive skills
- Course improved critical thinking
- Course improved connections with faculty
- Course improved connections with peers
- Course increased out-of-class engagement
- Course improved knowledge of campus policies
- Course improved knowledge of academic services
- Course improved managing time/priorities
- Course improved knowledge of wellness
- Sense of belonging/acceptance
- Usefulness of course readings
- Satisfaction with college/university
- Course included engaging pedagogy
- Overall course effectiveness

Additionally, the 2005 fall FYRST seminar group had statistically significant higher means on 12 of 15 student learning outcome factors as compared with other institutions having the same Carnegie classification as SRU. Institutionally, the 2005 fall FYRST seminar group had higher means on 10 of 15 student learning outcome factors as compared to last year's fall 2004 results.

The open-ended commentary by LCC/FYRST seminar faculty confirmed that the most valuable characteristics of the effort included: (a) students developed supportive peer relationships, (b) students seemed to interact/respond more often in class, and (c) students appeared to develop relationships with faculty more easily. Students reported that the most valuable characteristics of the effort included making friends, getting to know other students, and studying with other students.

National Survey of Student Engagement Data

The National Survey of Student Engagement (NSSE) further reveals improved student involvement and participation rates of Slippery Rock University students as compared to selected peer and Carnegie peer institutions. Of the five clusters identified by NSSE as benchmarks of effective educational practice, Slippery Rock University's 2005 NSSE results include:

- *Level of academic challenge.* SRU first-year and senior means were higher than selected and Carnegie peers.
- *Active and collaborative learning.* SRU first-year and senior means were higher than selected and Carnegie peers.
- *Student-faculty interaction.* SRU first-year and senior means were higher than selected and Carnegie peers.
- *Enriching educational experiences.* SRU first-year and senior means were equal to or higher than selected and Carnegie peers.
- *Supportive campus environment.* SRU first-year and senior means were higher than selected and Carnegie peers.

Various Program Survey Results

Assessment of the Faculty Resource site indicated improved frequencies of communication; enriched opportunities of relationship building; creation of high interest levels in using e-learning tools for other courses; and easy access of course materials for students, peer leaders, and faculty alike. Peer Leader program evaluations reflected student, peer leader, and faculty consensus that peer leaders: (a) understand first-year students' needs, (b) are a positive addition to the course, (c) are easier to relate to than to the professor, and (d) are helpful and could answer questions that faculty could not.

Conclusions

We believe that our institution's first-year initiative has been successful for the following reasons. First, the focus of our efforts has been on understanding the needs of our students. Second, we have continually strived to improve the quality of the academic and educational experiences throughout this process. Third, we have used assessment results of our programs and services to shape our future directions.

The integrated FYRST seminar, Learning Community Cluster, and Peer Leader program represent an initiative that has helped to change a campus culture. Best practices were not simply plugged into the university community and its programs. Rather, the aforementioned critical program characteristics were developed, shared, valued, and owned by constituency members university-wide. With a collective focus on successful student transitions, the FYRST/LCC program has empowered and mobilized faculty, administrators, and students in our institutional transformation effort—creating a wonderfully stimulating environment at "The Rock." The engagement of the campus community in this initiative has raised everyone's spirits—producing wonderful benefits for our first-year students.

References

Barefoot, B. O., & Gardner, J. N. (1993). The freshman orientation seminar: Extending the benifits of traditional orientation. In R. H. Mullendore, B. O. Barefoot, & D. S. Fidler (Eds.), *Designing successful transitions: A guide for orienting students to college* (Monograph No. 13, pp. 141-153).Columbia: University of South Carolina, National Resource Center for The Freshman Year Experience.

Gardner, J. N. (2001) Foreword. In S. L. Hamid (Ed.), *Peer leadership: A primer on program essentials* (Monograph No. 32, pp. v-viii). Columbia: University of South Carolina, National Resource Center for The First-Year Experience & Students in Transition.

Hunter, M. S., & Heath, M. M. (2001). The building blocks of the peer leader program: Recruitment, selection, and training. In S. L. Hamid (Ed.), *Peer Leadership: A primer on program essentials* (Monograph No. 32, pp. 37-52). Columbia: University of South Carolina, National Resource Center for The First-Year Experience & Students in Transition.

Primary Contributor

Jessamine Montero
Assistant Director, Act 101/FYRST Seminar Peer Leadership Coordinator
Slippery Rock University
Department of Academic Services
Bailey Library
Slippery Rock, PA 16057
Phone: 724-738-2687
E-mail: jessamine.montero@sru.edu

Additional Contributors

Cathy Brinjak
Director, Advisement Resources/FYRST Seminar & Learning Community Cluster Coordinator
Slippery Rock University

Connie Laughner-Ramirez
Director, Advisement Services/FYRST Seminar Peer Leadership Coordinator
Slippery Rock University

Amanda Yale
Associate Provost for Enrollment Services
Slippery Rock University

University of Michigan

Institution Profile

*Ann Arbor, MI
Public, Four-Year
"Linked"
Learning Communities*

Editors' Notes

The University of Michigan's Supreme Court case on affirmative action are just one indicator of an institutional commitment to diversity. The Michigan Community Scholars Program is another. Approximately 150 students participate each year in this residential learning community; approximately two thirds of them are first-year students, and the remainder are student leaders facilitating others' experiences. The enrollment is equally divided between African American and White students. While the university's overall retention rates for students of color are commendable, the Community Scholars Program has boasted 100% first-to-second-year return rates in recent years and serves as a model for colleges nationally.

The Institution

The University of Michigan is located in Ann Arbor, Michigan. It is a four-year, public, residential university. The undergraduate FTE is 24,446 with 6,115 first-year students, of whom 50.6% are women and 49.4% are men. Only 2% are over the age of 25. There are 68.4% White students. The total number of students of color equals 26.3%; 12.7% are Asian students, 7.6% are African American/Black students, 5% are Hispanic/Latino students, 1% are Native American students, and 5.2% race/ethnicity is unknown. Thirteen percent of the students are first-generation, including 6.2% of students with parents who have no college education, and 6.8% of students with parents who had some college education but no degree.

Description of the Initiative

The Michigan Community Scholars Program (MCSP) has tried to bring together, in one setting, some of the best features of engaged learning in undergraduate education by building a diverse, innovative scholarly community. In doing so, it hopes to support the academic success and retention rates of students from all backgrounds. MCSP also wants to develop a longstanding commitment to civic engagement and community service demonstrated through participation and leadership in students. Another objective is for students to gain knowledge and experience with people from different backgrounds and viewpoints and gain the skills to constructively engage one another and cross boundaries.

MCSP, a residential, living-learning program, first opened its doors to students in the 1999-2000 academic year. Each year, MCSP has approximately 150 students, about two thirds of whom are first-year college students. The remaining one third are peer advisors, peer mentors, resident advisors, and course facilitators who have returned to the program for a second year in a leadership role.

Students are invited to join MCSP on the basis of its emphasis on community service, academic excellence, leadership, diversity, and community. They are informed about small seminars and other course requirements, outstanding faculty, community service offerings, and the opportunity to make close friends with socially diverse, but like-minded peers committed to making a difference in the world. Although the program refers to itself as a "scholars" program, all students admitted to the University of Michigan are eligible for admission to MCSP regardless of their academic profile. It is not an honors program. The primary MCSP admission criteria are students' expressed commitment to and experience with community service and making a difference in the world, as well as their interest in MCSP and what they feel they can contribute to the program. Thus, students in the program are a self-selected group in terms of purpose and commitment, but not with regard to academic achievement, academic concentration, or political views. Students apply by writing a short essay to this effect, and all who represent these criteria are admitted, space permitting. Only a handful of students are denied admission to the program each year.

MCSP embraces diversity as a core program asset for personal, social, cognitive, and community development. The program encourages its students to actively engage one another across their different backgrounds and provides structures for them to learn to do so effectively. Over the past seven years, the program has consistently maintained about 50% students of color and international students and 50% White students. There is also a greater representation of out-of-state students in the program than is found on campus as a whole. Most students who enroll are from the liberal arts and engineering colleges (comparable to UM rates), and many go on to pursue degrees in business, pre-med, pre-law, liberal arts, and engineering.

The University of Michigan has long had a commitment to becoming a multicultural campus. Its U.S. Supreme Court case victory on affirmative action is the most recent and prominent example. The MCSP emphasis on diversity is institutionally supported, which helps make the University of Michigan a more diverse and intellectually exciting community. The relationship is reciprocal and reinforcing.

MCSP is built on the concept of boundary-crossing, because it engages academic and student affairs, academic disciplines, faculty and student divisions, as well as diverse student groups and the community. One objective is to bring together the whole for the good of the partners. For example, MCSP is funded and actively supported by the College of Literature, Science, and the Arts and university housing. Faculty come from disciplines across the liberal arts as well as from the professional schools and welcome the opportunity for interdisciplinary collaboration in teaching and research. As they work to build a scholarly community of faculty, students, and staff, faculty teach in classrooms and residence halls, hold office hours in the residence halls, and join students in the cafeteria. Diversity and intergroup relations are viewed as integral to student learning and enhancing the educational experience. They are placed at the center, not the margins, of the program's undergraduate educational initiatives. Service-learning is one of the key elements of the learning experience.

The mission statement of MCSP states the following as its goals:

1. Deep learning
   - Engagement with ideas
   - Ways of knowing
   - Transition to college
   - Academic success
   - Learning about community
2. Engaged community
   - A scholarly community
   - A safe and accepting environment
   - An involved, participatory community
   - A focus on the individual and the group

3. Meaningful civic engagement /community service-learning
   - High quality service-learning
   - Reflection
   - Leadership development
   - Sustainable partnerships
   - Long-term commitment
4. Diverse democracy, intercultural understanding and dialogue
   - A diverse community
   - Participation in intergroup dialogue
   - Commitment to strong democracy
   - Reflection on social justice
   - Model good practice

Research Design

To assess the impact of MCSP, research designs for program evaluation, retention, and long-term impact were developed. Thus far, we have been able to collect data on retention rates as well as program evaluation, including student satisfaction, documentation of program trends and activities, and anecdotal reports from participants. With more research funding, we hope future research will include the long-term impact of the program.

The program is currently in the process of collecting data on retention and persistence rates of MCSP student leaders who continue to live in the residential setting during their sophomore year or beyond. It is the program's impression that these students, because of their more extended involvement in MCSP, will have greater persistence and graduation rates than MCSP students who remain with the program for just one year.

MCSP has been recognized as a program that has characteristics—academic engagement, intergroup dialogue, and engagement across social diversity, engagement with the community through service-learning, and close academic and student affairs collaboration—that are believed to be critical to developing mentally and emotionally healthy college environments. At present only anecdotal evidence is available to support the strong retention data in this regard. The program, however, is working to develop a research design of pre- and posttests for MCSP students and control groups, including linkages to CIRP data, to assess the mental health of MCSP students in terms of depression, stress, and binge drinking.

Findings

For the past two consecutive years, 100% of underrepresented students of color who participated in MCSP as first-year college students returned to the university their sophomore year. The retention rate for all MCSP students each year was only a few percentage points lower than 100%. These MCSP rates surpass the overall University of Michigan persistence and retention rates. MCSP underrepresented students of color also have higher persistence rates than overall UM students.

MCSP also had considerable success in interrupting the cycle of racial segregation. Most MCSP students come from highly segregated neighborhoods and high schools. Through the efforts of faculty, staff, and student leaders, MCSP students go on to (a) live in diverse households, (b) participate and become leaders in multicultural organizations, (c) participate in academic experiences with an emphasis on ethnic/racial diversity, and (d) commit to community service and work with diverse populations after graduation.

Other indicators of success include:

- MCSP student leaders becoming campus-wide student leaders at UM well beyond their proportional numbers and particularly in areas of civic engagement and race/ethnic relations
- High rates of faculty retention in the MCSP program and interest from new faculty seeking to be a part of the program
- Ford Foundation grant to MCSP (as part of larger UM grant) on Difficult Dialogues: Religious Pluralism and Academic Freedom
- Creation of the Lives of Urban Children and Youth Initiative, sponsored by several academic units, but housed within MCSP
- Publication of a book, *Engaging the Whole of Service-Learning, Diversity, and Learning Communities* (Galura, Pasque, Schoem, & Howard, 2004), with co-authorship of articles by faculty, students, community partners, and staff
- MCSP highlighted on CNN's *Anderson Cooper 360* as a program that represents a counterexample to the resegregation of America

Conclusions

We have learned the following practices are critical to the ongoing success of MCSP.

1.   *Boundary-crossing and partnering with other units*, particularly between academic and student affairs units, takes patience, intentionality, and persistence.
2.   *Engaging one another across different backgrounds* requires sensitivity, intentionality, skills, and commitment.
3.   *The involvement of research faculty in a teaching program requires clear scholarly/professional benefits*, such as interdisciplinary collaboration, working with diverse students with a sense of purpose and commitment, and a community that strives to be the kind of scholarly community desirable for students choosing academia as a career.
4.   *Supportive, efficient, and careful use of faculty, staff, volunteers, and student leaders* is necessary to counter tight budgets and extremely tight schedules.
5.   *Developing good relations between the university and community* requires open communication, sustained commitment, and flexibility.

When MCSP was started, the University of Michigan already had a long history of support for residential learning communities, with collaboration between academic and student affairs. Equally important was Michigan's strong, public commitment to diversity and civic engagement. In addition, there were visible and respected academic and administrative champions for this kind of work at this institution. Finally, along with the University of Michigan's decentralized structure, a practice of giving support and a relatively wide degree of freedom to faculty who have good ideas has developed.

Many campuses have sought to adopt the MCSP program. While every institution is unique and must shape its own program to suit the particular features of its constituencies, mission, and culture, there are some suggestions that apply to most campuses.

First, it is critical to conceptualize with intentionality the goals of the program, including aspects such as the integration of various undergraduate initiatives, boundary-crossing practices, diversity, community, and academic achievement. Second, in regard to diversity, it must be understood that diversity serves an educational benefit for participants in the program, faculty, staff, and students alike. Diversity initiatives are truly successful only when they stand at the core of the program, not as add-ons. Third, although material and instrumental rewards matter, faculty interest and involvement in programs require primary attention to the intellectual benefits for faculty. Fourth, these programs need senior administrative and faculty champions in order to succeed.

Fifth, collaboration across academic affairs and student affairs will provide essential educational benefits, support, and funding for the program and its participants. Sixth, adequate support for the administrative leadership (faculty/staff) is critical in order to ensure program directors' extended appointments in these positions and resulting program stability. Seventh, student ownership and leadership of these programs are critical to the vitality, energy, ongoing innovation, and liveliness of the program. Eighth, attention to various aspects of community, including the scholarly, diverse, innovative, curricular and cocurricular community components, will bring cohesion, engagement, intellectual vitality, and commitment to the program. Finally, there must be high expectations for successful academic achievement and intellectual growth for each and every participant.

Reference

Galura, J. A., Pasque, P., Schoem., & Howard, J. E. (Eds.). (2004) *Engaging the whole of service-learning, diversity, and learning communities*. Ann Arbor, MI: OCSL Press.

Primary Contributor

David Schoem
Faculty Director, Michigan Community Scholars Program
The University of Michigan
1300 E. Ann Street
Ann Arbor, MI 48109-2050
Phone: 734-615-6847
E-mail: dschoem@umich.edu

Wagner College

Institution Profile

Staton Island, NY
Private, Four-Year
"Linked"
Learning Communities

Editors' Notes

The "Wagner Plan," now a decade old focused the college's faculty and students on broad but critical outcomes for a liberal arts education. Central to this was a three-tiered, mandatory learning community experience for all students, in their first and last year of study, and a year between. The emphases of the learning communities are "reading, writing, and doing," with the goals of enhancing critical analysis, communication, and observational skills; recognition of cultural diversity; and service to the community. Ongoing formative assessment led to the strengthening of the writing skills component of the learning communities. Institutionalization of the framework is evidenced in the position of a dean of experiential learning. Very substantial drops in DFW rates have been a result.

The Institution

Wagner College is located in the Staten Island borough of New York City. Wagner is a co-educational, private liberal arts college with professional programs, offering both bachelor's and master's degrees.

The undergraduate student population in fall 2006 was 1,876; of those 529 were first-year students. Resident students comprise 75% of the undergraduates. The percentage of women to men is roughly 60% to 40%; students of color are about 14% of the population. Approximately 30% of students are first-generation college students. Only 2% of students are nontraditional age.

Description of the Initiative

The Wagner Plan embraces the learning community concept, packaging thematically linked courses, and enrolling a common cohort of students. The educational benefits of learning communities are well documented. Students generally learn better in groups. They reinforce in- and out-of-class learning by creating social grouping within their common courses. Research on learning communities has shown significant increases in knowledge acquisition, problem solving, and enthusiasm for subject matter, and in retention and graduation rates.

The Wagner College faculty approved the Wagner Plan in October of 1997 and implemented it in the fall of 1998. The college changed from credits to units (36 units or courses required to graduate), and added requirements for three learning communities and experiential learning. The First Year Program (FYP) learning community includes two courses from different disciplines linked by a common theme and a third course, known as a Reflective Tutorial, which includes the experiential learning and writing intensive components. The second, or Intermediate Learning Community, combines two courses and again emphasizes interdisciplinary connections. The Senior Learning Community combines a capstone course in the major with a Reflective Tutorial and a more intensive experiential learning requirement. These learning communities are required of all students.

In the FYP, the Reflective Tutorial is a one-unit course. Reading and writing assignments are coupled with the learning community theme and directly connected to the semester's experiential learning assignment. Different from freestanding internships, reflective tutorials encase internships, fieldwork, and service-learning experiences within the context of "reading, writing, and doing." These experiences are directly related to the learning community theme and the two other disciplinary courses in which the common cohort of students are enrolled.

Full-time faculty teach the FYP learning community and serve as advisors to first-year students until they declare a major. Issues discussed in the Reflective Tutorial are adjustment to college, time management, college and community resources, information literacy, writing, and an introduction to issues of diversity. The use of peer tutors has been beneficial to both students and faculty. Each learning community is assigned a writing intensive tutor (WIT), who assists students in improving their writing skills, and a research intensive tutor (RIT), who helps students gain an understanding of the available information resources.

The major goals of the program are to begin the processes of liberal learning through (a) critical analysis; (b) improvement of reading, observational, and writing skills; (c) recognition of cultural diversity; and (d) service to the community.

The dean of learning communities and experiential learning is responsible for overseeing the learning communities and the experiential component. All contacts with the community-based organizations are secured through this dean's office. Monthly meetings of the FYP faculty and a yearly retreat are held to develop standards, discuss issues, conduct faculty development workshops, and review assessment data. The FYP faculty elect a faculty member to be the coordinator of the program.

A Sample Learning Community: "Connect with Art and History"

The learning community combining art history and history courses provided an excellent example of the development of the "reading, writing, and doing" elements of the curriculum. In a learning community originally called "Creativity and Conflict in Modern Times: The West in Global Context," the history and art history faculty members used a placement model where students interned at cultural sites, supplemented by two field trips to cultural institutions. The dean of experiential learning arranged placements, and faculty rarely had direct contact with site supervisors. While some students enjoyed interning at Ellis Island or the African Art Museum, others complained of being assigned clerical tasks. Even when placements were modified to have students in teams at each site, with some interning and some researching the civic, cultural, and economic aspects of each institution, results were not positive. Then, the faculty turned to a partnership model, placing all students at one site and designing a program that matched their students and partners' needs. The faculty were directly involved, and a more powerful program emerged (albeit more time-consuming for faculty, particularly in the start-up phase).

In the new learning community, "Connect with Art: A Literacy Project for Third Graders," the faculty matched the college's modern western civilization and art history curriculum with the New York State art and reading requirements for third-graders. In consultation with teachers at Public School 57 (a New York City elementary school), the faculty members chose 10 books and art projects related to colonial artist Benjamin West, Pablo Picasso, Faith Ringold's book on Martin Luther King, Jr. and others. Every Friday during the fall term, Wagner students worked with the entire third grade class (about 100 students or a 1:4 ratio) on reading, writing, and art projects. The final lesson brought the third-graders to the Wagner art gallery. The principal of P.S. 57 phoned the faculty after the first year of this experience with positive news: literacy rates in his five third-grade classes had soared as measured by city-wide reading tests, achieving the 15th-highest gain in the city.

While helping to build a foundation of literacy at the elementary level, Wagner students were making evocative intellectual, cultural, and civic connections. As they learned about impressionism, they taught lessons about Claude Monet as well as the Japanese artist Hokusai who inspired him. Further, students examined inequities in public schools, notably in arts-in-education, to spur advocacy. Lessons on art and history, in two courses common across many of the nation's colleges, were strengthened by a provocative and rewarding experiential context.

Research Design

The Wagner Plan for the Practical Liberal Arts was developed as a way to honor both the liberal arts and professional programs into which first-year students were entering by ensuring integration across disciplines, and the integration of in- and out-of-class learning. The purpose of the experiential learning component of the FYP was to provide an opportunity for reflection on the interplay of the liberal arts and practical experience, provide writing-intensive instruction, and increase students' engagement with the Staten Island and metro New York City community. The learning community format was intended to increase interaction between and among faculty and students, to address the integration of first-year commuter students with residential students, and to address issues of transition to college. As the program developed over the years, the goal of exposing first-year students to issues of diversity was added. Finally, a desired outcome of the First Year Program was to increase student retention from the first to second year.

Assessment methods used for formative and summative purposes included surveys of students and community site supervisors, reviews of writing samples, focus groups, and institutional data collection and analysis. The surveys of community site supervisors were useful for strengthening the meaningfulness of the time that students spent at the experiential sites. Site supervisor comments allowed faculty members to improve the in- and out-of-class connections in subsequent years.

Findings

Students were surveyed at the end of the first semester regarding their experience in the learning community (e.g., amount of interaction with faculty, amount of interaction with peers, challenge to improve communication skills, extent of course connection) and their experience with the experiential learning component (e.g., "My participation was beneficial to the site."; "The experience made the class material more meaningful."; "Experience improved problem solving ability."; "Experience increased understanding of civic responsibility."). Students were also surveyed at the end of the first year regarding their connections with students and faculty, the degree of interactivity within their courses, and exposure to diversity issues such as race, religion, economic status, gender, disability, and sexual orientation. Overall, the surveys showed increased participation, satisfaction, and connection from 1998 through 2004. For example, in 1998, 46% of students "agreed" or "strongly agreed" that the experiential learning component was beneficial; by 2004, the figure was 78%. Similarly, in 1998, 19% of students agreed or strongly agreed that the experiential learning component made the class material more meaningful; by 2004 that figure was 61%. In 1998, 53% of students agreed or strongly agreed that their community experience increased their sense of civic responsibility; by 2004, the response was 75%. Tracking the survey results from year to year and listening to feedback from students, site supervisors, and faculty provided encouragement and direction for program improvement.

A longitudinal writing assessment project began in 2001. Students' writing was collected over time and rated according to a college-wide rubric. Faculty from across the college, not just faculty teaching in the FYP, participated in the writing assessment. It was discovered that there was a lack of uniformity across FYP learning communities in terms of how much writing was being expected and being done. As a result, more faculty development devoted to writing was done within the FYP. The topic of plagiarism, raised during the writing assessment process, was referred to the academic honesty committee. Also, changes in how students were made aware of the academic honesty policy were implemented in following years. Faculty who participated in the writing assessment process also reported gaining ideas for writing better assignments and more effective drafting and peer (student) review techniques.

Other measures of program success were student enrollment and retention. In the fall of 1998, 438 new first-year students entered the college, and 77% persisted into their sophomore year. By the fall of 2003, the numbers had increased: 534 first-year students entered the college, and 90% persisted into their sophomore year. Fall 2004 numbers saw a slight dip: 491 first-year students entered, and 89% persisted.

In general, the results show that the students were energized, and many students became committed advocates of arts-in-education in public schools. Students commented:

"P.S. 57 was an eye-opening experience."
"Connect with Art was one of the most touching and changing experiences of my life."
"The children managed to shatter racial stereotypes in the media."
"They really changed my entire outlook on children."
"The kids taught me not to make any assumptions about people."

Conclusions

Taken together, the survey results, positive responses from faculty, and enrollment and retention numbers provided evidence of program success that more than justified the expenses of the program (i.e., faculty stipends for participation, expenses for faculty development workshops and retreats). In 2005, the college received the TIAA-CREF Theodore M. Hesburgh Award in recognition of the First Year Program and the accompanying faculty development components.

Critical Elements

A variety of elements were in place that contributed to the success of the initiative. A strength in the development of the FYP was that it was undertaken by the faculty and administration as a whole. It was implemented as a comprehensive program for all first-year students rather than as a pilot program for a subset of students. Aside from that context, which cannot always be replicated at other institutions, elements critical to the success of the program were faculty development and collaboration between student and academic affairs.

Faculty development was woven throughout the process and continues each year in monthly meetings and an annual FYP retreat. Topics for faculty development include writing instruction, academic advising, facilitating classroom discussion about diversity, and linking experiential learning within courses. At times, a consultant from outside the college was brought in to make a presentation; at other times faculty within the FYP presented in a best practices format.

The FYP was an ideal setting for collaboration between student and academic affairs. The Academic Advisement Center, staffed by a small number of professional advisors, worked closely with the faculty in the FYP because the faculty members were the primary advisors for their students. Academic Advisement Center staff supported faculty by providing information about student development and major exploration and about specific populations of students such as international students, students with disabilities, and student athletes. An annual campus-community event, "Celebrate Diversity," was developed in conjunction with student affairs administrators, faculty, and organizations across Staten Island and continues to involve not only first-year students as participants, but also upper-class students as organizers of the event. A final example of the close collaboration between faculty and student affairs administrators is the communication that occurs regarding the status of individual students. Faculty often notify administrators when students consistently miss classes. Notices are then sent to faculty if students have been hospitalized or some other emergency has occurred. This working relationship between faculty and college administrators helps the college reach out to students who are in jeopardy and in need of support.

Implications and Recommendations

It has been noted that Wagner College was somewhat unique in terms of the whole-heartedness with which the college embraced and implemented The Wagner Plan, and within that, the First Year Program. Beyond that, the implications and recommendations for other institutions are broadly applicable. The FYP was developed with clearly articulated learning goals: interdisciplinary linkages, experiential learning, intensive reflection and writing, and high levels of interaction between faculty and students. The college relied heavily on the plan and program in recruiting new students, and has seen changes in terms of increased numbers of applications and matriculants, and increased entry indicators such as SAT scores and high school grade point averages.

The appointment of a full-time administrator such as the dean of experiential learning was essential to the success of that part of the program, as she worked closely with faculty to find appropriate sites for all the first-year students, listened to feedback from faculty and site supervisors to improve the placements, coordinated transportation, and conducted the program assessment. As the First Year Program evolved, the dean worked closely with the faculty coordinator of the program to provide faculty development. The dean also provides consistency and oversight throughout the calendar year, which has been vital for the sustainability of the FYP.

Primary Contributor

Anne Goodsell Love
Dean of the College
Wagner College
1 Campus Road
Staten Island, NY 10301
Phone: 718-390-3423
E-mail: alove@wagner.edu

Additional Contributors

Julia Barchitta
Dean of Learning Communities
Wagner College

Lori Weintraub
Associate Professor of History
Wagner College

Ruta Shah-Gordon
Associate Dean for Student Development
Wagner College

Sirena LaBurn
college student
Wagner College

Wright State University

Institution Profile

Dayton, OH
Public, Four-Year
"Linked"
Learning Communities

Editors' Notes

The delivery of more personal instruction and guidance to first-year students is a challenge in this continuing era of budget cuts, increasing class sizes, and reductions in the percentage of full-time faculty. Moreover, pressures of "publish or perish" may lead faculty and administrators to believe that increased concentration by faculty on first-year students is in conflict with other institutional objectives. To counter these limitations, Wright State has turned to the use of peer instructors, or established undergraduate students, to lead or assist with first-year seminar courses. Beyond institutional and fiscal interests are the ideas that peer instructors may add inherent value that conventional instructors do not. Wright State's feedback from first-year students suggests that peer instruction can be at least as effective as alternatives, when sufficiently structured and closely monitored.

The Institution

A rich and dynamic community of nearly 17,000 students (13,000 are undergraduates), Wright State University-Dayton Campus was founded in 1964 and granted full university status in 1967 as the 12th state-assisted university in Ohio. Wright State is a nationally accredited, comprehensive, open admission, four-year public institution with 109 undergraduate degree programs and 46 graduate and professional degree programs. Wright State has six colleges and three schools including schools of medicine and professional psychology. Wright State was developed to provide access to higher learning to the city of Dayton and the surrounding counties. Most (93%) students are from Ohio: 85% White, 11% African American, 0.3% Asian, 1% Hispanic, and 0.3% Native American. Three thousand students live on campus, and 18% of the students are age 25 and over. Approximately 40% of the 3,752 first-year students are first generation (i.e., students whose parents have not earned a college degree).

Description of the Initiative

The University College at Wright State provides a comprehensive first-year experience that includes learning communities, academic advising, developmental education, tutoring, math learning assistance, writing assistance, standardized and placement testing, and new student orientation.

Learning communities at Wright State were officially inaugurated in 2000, but pilot programs have been taking place since the mid-1990s. The learning community (LC) program targets full-time, first-year students (i.e., traditional degree-seeking undergraduates who have earned fewer than 45 credit hours). The majority of these students have never been to college before; however, some first-year students have occasionally participated in the Post-Secondary Enrollment Option Program (PSEOP) in high school but have not completed all of their general education courses.

The program currently serves approximately 78% of first-year students who voluntarily enroll in a LC. A wide variety of learning communities are offered to incoming students, including theme-based, major-based, residential, and general college success learning communities.

Most Wright State learning communities include a cohort of 25 students who take two or more classes in common, such as psychology, sociology, or history, as well as the first-year seminar designed as the "home base" course.

The four major goals of the First-Year Experience/Learning Community program are to help first-year students (a) adjust to college, (b) achieve academic success, (c) develop personally, and (d) explore career development. The overarching theme is to ease the students' transition from high school to college by providing support, information, and guidance at one of the most critical times in their college careers.

The learning communities support in-class and out-of-class learning experiences. Faculty, staff, student groups, and academic units across the campus—including departments such as residence life, student activities, student support services, and judicial affairs—work together toward the learning community program's success. The collaboration has many benefits including introducing campus resources to new students and getting them involved in cocurricular activities. Instructors, for example, often bring guest speakers and student groups into the classroom as a way of introducing more campus resources to new students.

In the fall of 2000, 45 first-year seminar sections were offered, enrolling about 50% of the entering first-year students. By the fall of 2005, WSU offered 80 sections of the first-year seminar to serve 1,700 new students. To be able to offer all of these learning community courses, Wright State elicited the help of faculty and professional staff to teach. Most of the faculty members who teach first-year seminars come from the College of Liberal Arts and the College of Science and Math and teach major-based first-year seminars. Most professional staff instructors are University College advisors. Residence hall staff members teach residential living-learning communities, and other campus staff members often teach theme-based sections. Finally, to be able to manage the rapid expansion of the LC program, Wright State hired, carefully trained, and supervised juniors, seniors, and graduate students to serve as peer instructors (approximately 25-30 students) for some of the first-year seminar sections. These peer instructors are solo instructors who fulfill all of the teaching, grading, and mentoring requirements of this position.

The process for selecting peer instructors begins in February and March each year. In April, we interview applicants, and we make selections in May. Our program is open to rising juniors, seniors, and graduate students with a cumulative GPA of 2.7 or higher (3.0 preferred). We seek students with good communication skills, diversity awareness, and prior experience teaching or working with groups, first weekend/summer orientation programs, and/or student organizations.

Research Design

We turned to peer instruction because we needed to serve more students and had limited resources. However, we needed to find out if peer instructors were as effective as the staff instructors in teaching new students. In order to answer this question, Wright State compared student evaluations of peer and staff instructors for UVC101. Specifically, the assessment method was based upon questions on the Student Evaluation of Instruction, which is given to students in all Wright State courses, and the First-Year Seminar Evaluation, which is given to all students in UVC101. The First-Year Seminar Evaluation was developed by University College to assess the four major goals of the First-Year Experience/Learning Community program. In addition to assessing these goals, the evaluation also asks also asked students (a) if they would recommend a learning community and first-year seminar to other students and (b) if their participation in the learning community helped them make the transition from high school to college. Both evaluation forms ask students to indicate their level of agreement with several statements. Students indicate their preferences based on the following Likert scale (strongly agree = 5, agree = 4, neutral = 3, disagree = 2, and strongly disagree = 1). Therefore, a mean for a question could range from a low of 1 to a high of 5, with 3.0 being the midpoint. A mean of all student responses combined for the sections taught by peer instructors was compared with the equivalent mean of all student responses for sections taught by staff instructors. This was done for two quarters, fall 2004 and fall 2005.

Findings

The means for UVC101 students taught by peer instructors and for those UVC101 students taught by staff instructors for fall 2004 and fall 2005 are broken out by seven statements selected for comparison (Table 1). For the 2004 data for "class time was well spent," the peer instructors' mean of 4.58 was higher than the 4.21 mean for the staff instructors. Although in 2005 this difference decreased (4.32 for peers compared to 4.21 for staff), the peer instructors again had the higher student ratings. In total, the peer instructors' means were above the staff means (although not always by much) for 12 of the 14 questions.

Table 1
Student Response Mean Scores for Evaluations of Peer and Staff Instructors

	2004 (*n* = 906)		2005 (*n* = 904)	
	Peers Group Mean	**Staff Group Mean**	**Peers Group Mean**	**Staff Group Mean**
Wright State standard Evaluation statement				
Class time was well spent.	4.58	4.21	4.32	4.21
I learned a lot from the instructor in this course.	4.30	4.07	4.24	4.12
I was challenged in this course.	3.40	3.16	3.27	3.11
Coming into this course I was motivated to learn this subject.	3.72	3.68	3.66	3.59
First-Year Seminar Evaluation Statement				
I would recommend being in an Learning Community and first-year seminar to other new students.	4.14	4.04	3.83	4.03
Being in a LC and first-year seminar my first quarter helped me make the transition from high school to college.	3.87	3.79	3.72	3.79
At least one activity in this class helped me to better appreciate the diversity of people at WSU and/or in the world.	4.23	3.95	4.13	4.12

First-year students may need to seek out upper-class students as mentors and thus may respond more favorably to instructors closer to their age in a course focused on adjustment to college, leading to higher means for peer instructors. Peer instructors' stronger areas could also be attributed to the required peer instructor training that takes place throughout the summer and continues into the quarter. Peer instructors also have weekly supervision seminars to discuss how their classes are going and to share and receive suggestions from the director and returning peer instructors. The amount of training and structure given to peer instructors allows them to focus more time on working with students on an individual basis, while gaining the experience of teaching a college-level course. Staff members who teach our first-year seminar courses are given a master syllabus and guidelines but do not receive the same amount of individual and group support and structure that peer instructors receive. Thus, the use of upper-class and graduate students as solo peer instructors in learning communities is allowing an increase in the quantity of sections offered, while still maintaining the quality of the experience as perceived by the new students themselves.

Conclusion

Several elements were critical to the success of the peer instructor program. There was ongoing support from the provost and the vice president for curriculum and instruction/dean of University College for using students as peer instructors to expand the LC program. This high level of support made it easier to expand and involve other departments in the success of the program. Secondly, as other academic departments became aware of the LC program we were able to recruit upper-class and graduate students interested in teaching as a career as well as those who wanted the experience of working with first-year students. This opportunity continues to be beneficial for academic departments, because many of these students teach a first-year seminar for students interested in their major focus (e.g., business, early childhood education, psychology). Third, the development of a quality five-day summer training program, which included a variety of course materials and helpful resources, prepared the peers to be effective seminar instructors. As stated above, the requirements for peer instructors are more stringent than for staff instructors, and the director of the LC program trains and monitors the peers to meet these requirements. For example, the peer instructors' syllabi were reviewed to ensure that each one was following the master syllabus. Small, weekly group supervision meetings were also initiated to discuss issues that could arise throughout the term. Finally, the director of the LC program kept an "open door" policy and helped peer instructors as needed.

We have learned that peer instructors are an invaluable asset to our learning community program. The director of learning communities along with the graduate teaching assistant for learning communities provided a Wright State-specific learning communities supplement called "Into the Water." This supplement is a collection of materials and activities that can be used in-class by instructors of all first-year seminar courses. This supplement will be updated yearly as new materials and new ideas are presented by peer instructors and Wright State University staff each fall. We plan to continue our present training program and will continue to provide more resources such as videos, list of guest speakers, and supplements to make their experience even more valuable. As we expand our learning community program past fall quarter into winter and spring, we expect our peer instructors will continue to be an invaluable asset.

Implications and Recommendations

Other institutions could implement a peer instructor program to teach first-year seminars by seeking support and resources from senior leadership at the institution. It is critical to carefully select and train the peers and to continue to support them throughout their teaching. While this involves training many new instructors each year to replace students who graduate, it allows an increase in the number of sections of first-year seminar courses offered at a very modest cost while maintaining the quality of the experience for new students.

Primary Contributor

Edwin B. Mayes
Director of the First Year Experience
University College
180 University Hall
Wright State University
3640 Colonel Glenn Highway
Dayton, OH 45435
Phone: 937-775-5750

Additional Contributors

Doug Saul
Director of Learning Communities
Wright State University

Heather Schilling-Beckett
Graduate Teaching Assistant
Learning Communities
Wright State University

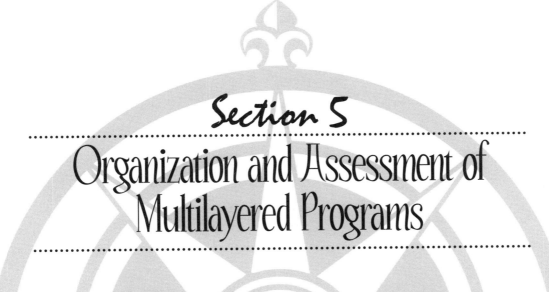

Section 5
Organization and Assessment of Multilayered Programs

Montclair State University

Institution Profile

*Montclair, NJ
Public, Four-Year
Organization and
Assessment of Multilayered
Programs*

Editors' Notes

The most critical aspect of a holistic approach to the first college year is the coordination of programs and services across campus. Montclair State University has tackled that challenge through an oversight department called New Student Experience. The model represents an organizational structure that has been recognized externally for its multifaceted design, collaborative culture, and intentional integration of the curriculum and cocurriculum. Collection and use of both direct and indirect measures provides evidence of the impact on multiple levels of learning and development.

The Institution

Montclair State University (MSU) is a comprehensive four-year public university in Montclair, New Jersey. It is currently the second largest and fastest growing university in the state. In fall 2005, its full-time undergraduate enrollment experienced a 4% increase, reaching 12,174. Its first-time, full-time enrollment increased 8.7% and reached an all time high of 1,907, accounting for 57% of all new students. Approximately 55% of the first-year students are residential, while about 45% are commuters.

MSU enjoys a wide array of ethnic and socioeconomic diversity within its student body. In fall 2005, approximately 97% of its first-time, full-time first-year students were NJ residents, with 71% from six of the surrounding counties. These counties vary in their ethnic make-up, family income, and parental educational attainment. According to MSU's 2005 CIRP data, nearly 25% of the first-year class reported that their mothers and fathers had earned college degrees, and an additional 11% of mothers and 13% of fathers earned graduate degrees. The reported ethnicity of the first-year class is as follows: White 62%, Hispanic 19%, African American 11%, Asian 7%, and international 1%. Like many other campuses, women outnumbered men in the fall 2005 cohort, 57% compared with 43%, respectively.

Description of the Initiative

New Student Experience (NSE) has evolved into a truly comprehensive department since it was created in 1997. Its curricular and cocurricular initiatives have been purposefully designed to allow first-year students to connect with a supportive network of peers, faculty, and staff. Over the years, the department's individual activities have been examined and then closely integrated to develop a holistic approach to promoting first-year student retention. Through this design, which I term "webbing," NSE's initiatives have become interconnected using a combined set of resources and strategies. This approach has been greatly supported by the university's upper administration, which values collaboration and innovation.

NSE was initially designed to conduct new student orientation, transfer orientation, welcome week activities, the first-year seminar, counseling, workshops, and living-learning communities for undeclared students and those majoring in programs in the College of Humanities and Social Sciences. Housed in the Dean of Students Office in the Division of Student Development and Campus Life, NSE serves all new students, which include first-time, first-year and transfer students.

As MSU's enrollment grew, the university decided to be more intentional in improving its first-year retention rate. In 1999, NSE became part of a newly created area of the division, enrollment management, and the department focused on maintaining a small school feel for a larger first-year class. In 2000, NSE launched a first-year advisement program, expanded its learning communities to serve both resident and commuter students, and enhanced its peer leadership program to do outreach during the academic year. These efforts have helped NSE monitor student performance and promote engagement.

The seminar became a general education requirement in 2002, leading to an increase in the number of sections offered from 19 in 2001 to 63 in 2002. Despite its administrative location, NSE has continued to maintain full responsibility for all aspects of the course. NSE partnered with the faculty and chairs of several additional majors during this period to expand the learning communities program and linked the seminar to these communities.

Examples of the Webbing Conceptual Model Introduced in 2004

NSE's First Year Counselors (FYCs) facilitate two-day overnight new student orientation (NSO) programs during the summer with each event serving approximately 300 students. Through the support of numerous campus partners in both academic and student affairs, NSO serves to better align students' expectations of the social pressures and academic demands they might encounter on a college campus. The family orientation program runs on the first day of the student program with roughly 125 attendees per event. Families have several opportunities throughout the day to connect with faculty and administrators to learn more about the resources and academic programs on campus. Peer leaders play a significant role in educating students and family members about the transition to college. Intensive training sessions on ethics, diversity, university policies, campus resources, peer advisement, and interpersonal communication are held in the spring and summer to prepare them for orientation. In the fall, the peer leaders work with the FYCs and conduct outreach to the students they meet over the summer.

All first-year students are assigned to a FYC who assists them with major exploration, academic advisement, campus integration, and personal growth. Potential at-risk students are identified by FYCs through an early intervention program done in partnership with the new student seminar instructors. In the spring, the FYCs monitor probation students on their caseload using an intrusive advisement and referral program.

The First Year Success Series (FYSS) also webs together a few of NSE's activities. It is a calendar of events developed with campus partners that address first-year transition issues. Specific programs are held in the residence halls for resident students. The FYSS supports the new student seminar, which requires students to attend FYSS events and write reaction papers on their experiences. In addition, the FYCs refer probation students on their caseload to FYSS events that address skill development and coping strategies.

As the university has grown, so have the number of new student seminar sections. Approximately 70 sections of the seminar were offered in fall 2006. This one-credit course fulfills the first-year seminar general education requirement. Its curriculum focuses on the academic, social, and personal development of first-year students. As indicated, the course has become another vehicle for webbing, connecting NSE's probation initiatives and the FYSS.

NSE coordinates a large learning communities program, connecting college writing, new student seminar, and two general education or major courses (10 credits). NSE works with academic deans and department chairs annually to design and evaluate the learning communities. These communities vary in their levels of faculty coordination and collaboration within the schools and colleges.

Research Design

Although the university's first-year enrollment has steadily grown, its infrastructure has not increased at the same rate. The university's administration is very forward thinking and ambitious and aspires to significantly raise its first-year retention rate and its enrollment. As MSU is committed to maintaining a small school feel, this gap presents a challenge. In response, and using limited resources, NSE developed a set of interconnected strategies and integrated them into the fabric of the campus. An assessment-driven management plan was also launched to monitor NSE's progress toward goal attainment.

A number of assessment tools were used to capture information regarding the programs. Surveys were administered to new student and family orientation attendees and analyzed after each program. In addition, the First-Year Initiative (FYI) Assessment survey was administered, and institutional data were used to track students in the learning communities in regard to persistence and GPA. Finally, probationary students were asked to complete self-evaluations to determine areas of challenge.

Findings

Our data indicate that approximately 90% of the family attendees and approximately 85% of the student attendees positively rated their overall orientation experience. This feedback is being reviewed to plan for next year's orientation programs.

Regarding probationary students, in January 2004, 14% of the regularly admitted students were placed on probation, many of whom were residential students. The self-evaluations revealed that their obstacles were mostly nonacademic. Similar results were found the following year, confirming that nonacademic obstacles tend to be the predominant cause of poor academic performance among probation students. In fact, more than 90% of these students had SAT scores and high school GPAs that placed them in the "candidate for admission" category and did not possess any preadmission "red flags" identifying them as at-risk applicants. Preventative efforts were introduced, which contributed to a 2% reduction in the probation rate in spring 2006. A fall peer leader outreach initiative was introduced and a residential component was added to the First Year Success Series. In fall 2005, an early monitoring program was piloted, which served as a basis for the program currently operating through the new student seminar, resulting in 82% of the referred students earning above a 2.0 GPA.

The FYI has been used to identify areas of the seminar to develop and maintain. In 2005, the Usefulness of Course Readings factor was the top predictor of overall course effectiveness, contributing to the selection of a new text to better support the course curriculum. The 2006 instructor training sessions focused on pedagogy development based on the Course Included Engaging Pedagogy factor being the top predictor of course effectiveness.

Learning community tracking data for the 2004 cohort demonstrates the impact of the program on first-year student performance. Participants outperformed their eligible non-participant counterparts in GPA and persistence (completion of all attempted credits) during fall 2004. In addition, their retention rate was 5.1% higher than that of the comparison group. Because of these results, the program expanded into other majors, producing similar outcomes. More majors are now involved this academic year and plans are underway for further expansion in fall 2007.

Survey results demonstrate that participation has positively contributed to our students' transition to MSU, their ability to draw connections between the content of their courses, and their formation of peer relationships. Approximately 82% responded positively to the statement, "If I had to do it over again, I would choose to be in a learning community."

Conclusions

NSE's campus-wide initiatives have contributed to the university's successes. MSU has participated in the Consortium for Student Retention Data Exchange (CSRDE) for several years. Recognized by CSRDE for being a moderately selective public university that performs like a selective university, MSU has outperformed its peer institutions in its first-year student retention rate and its six-year graduation rate. The CSRDE 2004-2005 report demonstrates that while moderately selective public peer institutions had an average first-year retention rate of 74.1%, MSU's rate was 83.9% for its 2003 cohort. Furthermore, MSU's six-year graduation rate was 56.8% for its 1998 cohort, outperforming the rate of its peer moderately selective public institutions, which had an average six-year graduation rate of 45.6%.

The Association of American State Colleges and Universities (AASCU) sent a team to campus in spring 2005 to study factors contributing to the university's comparatively high outcomes for its 1998 and 2003 cohorts. The study team found NSE to be "an organizational structure for organizing a seamless first-year experience" (AASCU Study Team, 2005) and highlighted the department's multifaceted approach, the intentionality of its services, its collaborative spirit, and the integrated design of its initiatives.

MSU has centralized many of its services for first-year students through NSE. Frontloading has proven to be an effective means for MSU to achieve its comparatively high first-year retention rate. The webbing model offers NSE a structure in which service delivery becomes purposeful and efficient, and initiatives are logically connected to one another. When considering the challenge of serving an ever-growing first-year class with limited resources, the webbing model makes the goal of increasing the first-year retention rate more attainable.

The first step to implementing the webbing model was to develop a calendar of critical dates for its assessment activities. These data have been regularly evaluated to determine their impact, to correct and redirect where needed, and discover correlations. Making ongoing assessment and evaluation integral to NSE's mission has been critical to maintaining and sustaining funding and campus-wide collaborative support. The practice has contributed to the integrated nature of our campus-wide initiatives. By demonstrating our outcomes, NSE has been able to implement both curricular and cocurricular initiatives with the buy-in and participation of faculty and academic administrators. Developing and maintaining these relationships is essential because they serve as the foundation for our campus-wide initiatives and our students' success.

With the pressure of accountability looming, NSE must be attentive to its outcomes. NSE responded to these expectations in fall 2005 when the staff developed a five-year strategic plan containing measurable goals and associated action plans that are consistent with the university's mission. NSE's regularly scheduled assessment activities are embedded in the plan as they are critical to the evaluation process. The associated action plans correspond to a timeline for the completion of these activities. This level of staff involvement was important in allowing staff to make their own contributions to the plan's overall design and our common achievements.

The model described here is easily adaptable to nearly any program or institution that is confronted with the challenge of doing more with less. It requires that administrators carefully evaluate their units and pose the following questions: "What do we need to keep doing? How can we do a better job at what we do? What do we need to stop doing? Who do we need to be working with for our students to get the biggest bang for their bucks?" By regularly maintaining program data, these questions have become easier to answer within the department and to respond to when posed by constituents. The model also offers a framework from which to innovate, integrate, and bring order to seemingly uncontrollable circumstances. Furthermore, it requires the full involvement and participation of staff to brainstorm and collaborate and encourages us to look at our organizational structures in entirely different ways.

Reference

AASCU Study Team. (2005, March). *Graduation rate outcomes study campus visit*. Montclair, NJ: Montclair State University.

Primary Contributor

Michele Campagna
Director of New Student Experience
Montclair State University
1 Normal Avenue
Montclair, NJ 07042
Phone: 973-655-5369
E-mail: campagnam@mail.montclair.edu

University of Minnesota

Institution Profile

*Minneapolis, MN
Public, Four-Year
Organization and
Assessment of Multilayered
Programs*

Editors' Notes

Acknowledged risk factors in college success are being a first-generation college student and being low-income. Too often, these factors are found at a large university where the odds of isolation and anonymity could be heightened. This University of Minnesota program has survived substantial restructuringy, including the elimination of the General College. A clear mission and evidence of effectiveness are no doubt a part of this successful transition.

The Institution

The University of Minnesota, Twin Cities campus is a large, public land-grant research institution with a total undergraduate population of 28,957. Approximately 80% of the students are White; almost 17% are students of color (9.3% Asian American, 4.5% African American, 2.1% Chicano/Latino, 0.8% Native American) with 1.6% international students, and 2.4% unknown. There are 5,305 first-year students, and 28.2% of them are first-generation students.

Description of the Initiative

The University of Minnesota, Twin Cities is providing the foundation for the new first-year program that will begin in fall 2008. The institution is becoming more selective and, as a result, is expecting much quicker academic progress and higher undergraduate success rates, while investing heavily in raising the reputation of the university through research. As part of these changes, the university has decided to close the program called the General College (GC) and develop a learning community approach for TRIO students, called the Multicultural Learning Community (MLC).

Many faculty and staff from the General College have become part of a new academic unit called the Department of Post-Secondary Teaching and Learning (PSTL), housed in the College of Education and Human Development. First-year learning communities will be a signature component of this new department and will fall under a new moniker—The First Year Experience Program. During the 2007-2008 transition year, PSTL will offer approximately 28 learning communities to incoming first-year students. In 2008, the First Year Experience Program will serve all first-year students enrolled in the College of Education and Human Development program. The MLC learning community has been a model used to shape this initiative.

The MLC was specifically designed for first-year, first-generation college students who are also participants in the TRIO Student Support Services Program. The TRIO program, a federally funded initiative, provides intensive advising, leadership opportunities, and learning community or Supplemental Instruction courses to approximately 234 first-generation, low-income students and students with disabilities. For this program, first-generation students are defined as those whose parents do not have a four-year degree. The design of the MLC was in specific response to the access needs of students who have been historically marginalized on college campuses.

Research demonstrates that due to a series of factors including academic and economic constraints, low-income, first-generation students are less likely to persist and graduate from college compared to their traditional counterparts (Warburton, Bugarin, &Nunez, 2001). In addition, these students often feel more isolated because they have little preparation or understanding of the academic milieu (London, 1989; Rendon, 1996). This isolation is coupled with feeling marginalized by mainstream curricula that does little to reflect the life-worlds of these students (Jehangir, 2004). Furthermore, isolation and marginalization is heightened by gaps between services provided by student affairs and curriculum offered in academic courses.

The multicultural learning community included three classes based on the themes of *identity*, *community*, and *agency*. We focused on the social, cultural, and cognitive bridges that our themes enabled students to build between their personal and academic lives. This linkage allowed our students to (a) challenge and support each other in their learning, (b) apply diverse theories of multiculturalism to their lived experiences, (c) examine relationships among various mediums of expression and ways of knowing, and (d) find their own voices as agents of social change.

Each instructor took a different approach to teaching. In Multicultural Relations, students worked in a seminar format and small groups to examine issues of class, race, gender, disability, and homophobia in America. In the writing lab, students helped each other strengthen their abilities to participate and reflect upon the processes of academic writing and to understand how their writing relates with their peers. In the creativity art lab, students collaborated to create a final project, either a performance or a mural that expressed the themes of identity, community, and agency. This intentional connection of interdisciplinary courses allowed students to examine multicultural perspectives and link it with their experiences and learning community pedagogy.

This collective case study considers the problem of isolation and marginalization of first-generation college students through the lens of critical pedagogy. This approach considers ways in which a multicultural learning community can create a climate of academic and social integration (Tinto, 1997) to support the persistence of at-risk students. Rather than looking at retention as a summative outcome, we examined the formative pieces that underlie the nature of persistence and considered the *processes* by which the MLC might help students feel supported, engaged, and self-sufficient during their first year of college. The goals of the First Year Experience Program are to:

1. Develop a strong sense of belonging to the learning community and to the university as a whole.
2. Develop a repertoire of ways to think about and express ideas, emotions, and experiences.
3. Develop the ability to work collaboratively with others.
4. Bring lived experience into the classroom and explore connections between the academic community and other communities to which the students belong (e.g., home, religious, ethnic).
5. Strengthen self-efficacy by learning more about themselves as individuals and as members of the community.

The MLC was offered seven times between fall 2001 and 2007, and each time the enrollment was limited to 20 students per cohort. Given that the intended audience was low-income and first-generation students, registration for the MLC was managed by the advising staff in the TRIO Student Services Program. Students were presented with the option of registering for this learning community during orientation and registration meetings. If selected, they were provided with permission numbers that would allow them to register concurrently for all three courses. Whenever possible, particularly in the fall semester, the same advisor was assigned to all the students in the MLC.

Research Design

The primary question driving this study is: What is the experience of first-year, first-generation college students in a multicultural learning community at a predominantly White public research university? Our research design seeks to capture the process of students' experience during the semester and triangulates these findings by providing summative data at the end of the semester in the form of both focus groups and an electronic survey.

We employed a collective interpretive case-study method. All data collection required human subjects approval, and students signed a consent form. The primary data for this case study are comprised of personal documents including students' weekly learning logs, academic papers, reflective writing, and art projects from all three courses. In this collective case study, our intent is to capture the stories, experiences, and voices of the participants as they are participating in the learning community. All the data was transcribed and coded by a principal investigator and a second reader for validity.

Focus groups were conducted for the fall 2004 cohort and were held after the fall semester so that students would have some distance from the classes. The focus groups were conducted by student services staff and a graduate research assistant. The discussions were audio taped and later transcribed and coded.

In an effort to triangulate the data collection process, the last two MLC cohorts (fall 2004 and fall 2005) were asked to also complete a computer-based survey about their participation in the learning community at the end of the semester. The survey was adapted from The Learning Communities Student Questionnaire developed at Temple University. We changed the survey slightly by asking students both *how often* they performed certain tasks and *how helpful* tthose tasks were to students' learning. The survey questioned students about in-class interactions, curricular connections, peer learning, socialization, communication with teachers, and out-of-class activities.

Findings

Based on the context of the five goals for the First Year Experience Program, our findings included:

1. Develop a strong sense of belonging to the learning community and to the university as a whole. Very quickly, most students lost their initial shyness with each other, showed a sense of group cohesion, and became comfortable exploring difficult topics and experiences. They began to see themselves as college students who were dealing with important ideas. When asked in a focus group how this openness was developed, a student replied,

> I think the community itself helped. We all got comfortable with each other so quick that we just, whatever spoke out.... And it was just like it gives you that feeling like I have known you so long I can say whatever comes to my mind.

The bonds in the class also extended beyond the classroom: "We would actually stay after and go out to eat after classes and keep discussing it." In addition, several social events helped students identify with the learning community.

2. Develop a repertoire of ways to think about and express ideas, emotions, and experiences. The different disciplines in the learning community gave students many opportunities to practice a broad range of ways to construct and represent knowledge. Students made connections among the curriculum in different ways. For some, the connections were very specific. Other students were able to make thematic connections between the issues raised in each class. Still others found relationships between curriculum and their own lived experiences. One of the most important ways that students learned about different ways of making sense of the world was through their interactions with other students. For many students, it seemed to be a revelation that people think about things in different ways. A number of students wrote about this new awareness:

I was intrigued at what other people would say to what they wrote. It was very interesting that people could come up with two totally different things from looking at the same picture. It shows that art can be looked at in very different ways and it depends a lot on where a person grew up or what their heritage is.

3. Develop the ability to work collaboratively with others. Throughout the semester, the class activities emphasized collaboration. There were multiple opportunities for students to engage in whole-class critical discussions, give presentations, and engage in peer reviews. Students quickly took on the roles of co-teachers and learners. Students also learned to critique each other and demonstrated an understanding of their own learning style preferences.

Although the disagreements and ambiguity was often frustrating to students, it gave them first-hand experience in what it means to participate in a democratic, collaborative learning community. The way in which students managed this ambiguity was through reflection of their different learning style preferences and development:

I think every aspect of this group presentation was good and helped my learning. Considering the fact that I was hearing from my fellow students—in some ways, I think that is really effective way of teaching compared to [just] a professor standing in front teaching. I don't really have anything against any of my professors, but sometimes it's just good to hear from another person; especially your classmates who took their time, researched, and prepared a presentation

4. Bring lived experience into the classroom and explore connections between the academic community and the other communities. Many of the class assignments asked students to make connections between their own experiences, education, and viewpoints and the more academic language, theories, and issues discussed in class. The assignments honored students' voices at the same time that they enabled students to develop greater fluency in academic discourse. In an effort to create a bridge between the students' academic and social experience, the MLC included extracurricular activities such as trips to a museum and plays that reflected multicultural perspectives.

I've really enjoyed looking at the Chicano art. Most of the paintings showed the struggles and the lives of the Chicano people. [In one painting] there were 16 faces, and I could see myself in one of those faces.

5. Strengthen feelings of self-efficacy by learning more about themselves as individuals and as members of the community. Students discussed their feelings of self-efficacy, both with regard to a heightened sense of self-awareness and pride in themselves, as well as a new awareness of

their academic identity and their voice and contributions as learners. One student articulated the importance of being part of knowledge construction rather than a passive recipient of learning:

> The way I look at things is a lot different, I would say more mature. [I]n high school you would think the way your friends do or the way you're are told to. But now whenever [the professor] asks questions it isn't something from the book, it was what do you think? And I have never been asked that...

Multiculturalism and Belonging

Students began to consider the value of heterogeneity in the learning process. Not only did they say that they value hearing many ideas and disciplinary contexts, they also came to understand that hearing from many different people broadened their perspective:

> I have never worked with so many different races and backgrounds on anything like this and it was very special for me because I have learned that our arguments and conversations is made up of our experiences and it has a lot to do with who we are.

The process of developing a sense of belonging takes time. The multicultural curriculum fostered opportunities for students to connect their school and home worlds, and in doing so, they often were able to better understand the lived experience of their peers.

Research Findings

The survey asked students about in-class interactions, curricular connections, peer learning, socialization, and communication with teachers. Of the 82 respondents, 96% reported listening to their peers on a weekly basis or every class, and 83% found this process to be helpful to their learning. Seventy-six percent of respondents indicated they engaged in activities that gave them a better sense of their identity weekly or in every class, and 75% indicated that this was helpful to them as learners. Finally, when respondents were asked how often they learned from students of cultural backgrounds different from their own, 87% reported that this occurred weekly or in every class, and 85% reported finding this helpful.

Conclusions

There are specific implications that might guide other programs in assessing needs and shaping learning community designs on different campuses. First, consider cognitive and affective factors such as identity in programmatic designs that impact persistence. The data from student reflections and focus groups suggest that how a student might feel in the classroom or group experience could impact the extent to which they engage in the academic work. Students' sense of belonging or validation can be a central motivator in their willingness to take the risk of contributing to the classroom discussion or expressing their ideas in an assignment.

Second, and closely connected to this, is building tangible bridges between students' personal lives and their academic lives. Critical thinking is a valuable outcome of the learning experience and finding ways to encourage students to apply theoretical perspectives to their own lived experiences makes it tangible. When we invite students to examine their own experiences and those of their peers, in context of ideas, positions, and disciplinary perspectives, we introduce conflict and ambiguity as part of the challenge of the learning process. Navigating through conflicting ideas plays an important role in students' ability to analyze, synthesize, and teach each other. It also empowers students to see themselves as knowledge bearers rather than simply receivers of knowledge.

Third, developing curricular and cocurricular expectations that require students to take ownership of their classroom experience so that the role of identity, diversity, and knowledge construction is extended into learning experience. True community does not simply occur—it is built consciously and with collective input.

References

Jehangir, R. (2004). *In their own words: The experience of first-year, first-generation college students in a multicultural learning community.* University of Minnesota. Unpublished dissertation.

London, H. B. (1989). Breaking away: A study of first-generation college students and their families. *American Journal of Higher Education, 97*(1), 144-170.

Rendón, L. (1996). Life on the border. *About Campus, 1*(5), 14-20.

Tinto, V. (1997). Classrooms as communities: Exploring the educational character of student persistence. *Journal of Higher Education, 68*(6), 599-623.

Warburton, E., Bugarin, R., & Nunez, A. M. (2001). *Bridging the gap: Academic Preparation and post secondary success of first-generation college students.* Washington, DC: National Center for Educational Statistics.

Primary Contributor

Rashné Jehangir
Assistant Professor
Department of Postsecondary Teaching and Learning
The University of Minnesota
140 Appleby Hall
128 Pleasant Street S.E.
Minneapolis, MN 55455
Phone: 612-625-3551
E-mail: jehan001@umn.edu

Additional Contributors

Patrick Bruch, Associate Professor
Department of Postsecondary Teaching and Learning
The University of Minnesota

Patricia James, Associate Professor
Department of Postsecondary Teaching and Learning
The University of Minnesota

Section 6
Designing and Assessing
First-Year Seminars

Concordia University

Institution Profile

St. Paul, MN
Private, Four-Year
Designing and Assessing
First-Year Seminars

Editors' Notes

While still a relatively new initiative, Concordia University's comprehensive approach to planning, assessment, professional development, and coordinated implementation of their first-year seminar is particularly noteworthy. The description of critical elements and lessons learned provide a clear and replicable process, for all types of institutions.

The Institution

Concordia University, St. Paul is a four-year private Lutheran university. There is a diverse student body of residential and commuter students in the traditional undergraduate programs. The number of FTE undergraduate students enrolled at Concordia in fall 2005 was 789 with 54% female and 46% male students. The racial/ethnic makeup included 69% White students, 10% African American students, 6.5% Asian/Pacific Islander students, 3% multiracial students, 2% Hispanic students, and 9.5% undisclosed.

The number of first-year students enrolled in the fall of 2005 was 165. Of the first-year students, 1% of these students were over age 25, and 28.5% were first-generation. We define first-generation college students by using the data from the FAFSA. Students are first-generation if (a) both parents are listed as high school or below as the highest degree or (b) only one parent is listed as high school or below as the highest degree and the other is listed as unknown.

Description of the Initiative

Concordia University offered the First-Year Seminar (FYS) for the second time in the fall of 2006. The major objectives of this initiative were developing common learning outcomes, creating assessment tools, implementing the assessment of the learning outcomes, and using the assessment results for course improvement and enhancement. A group of 12 faculty members at Concordia University, St. Paul, interested in offering a first-year experience for our students, developed a set of learning outcomes based on three principles: advising, building community, and enhancing academic skills. The program is organized to encourage faculty to increase the use of educational practices that are empirically linked with high levels of learning and development and to increase students' engagement in their learning. Our first-year seminar model links first-year seminar learning outcomes with our assessment tools. The course itself is an academic seminar with variable content. First-year seminar faculty created common learning outcomes that provided the framework for the seminar. These learning outcomes included the following: (a) to explore the academic community and develop new mentoring relationships with faculty, staff, and peers; (b) to experience the academic world through the community, intellectual inquiry, and relationships; (c) to evaluate sources of information, seeking answers to personal and intellectual questions; and (d) to express ideas by clearly articulating thoughts in written and oral forms of communication. The creation of the common learning outcomes was an important component of this initiative.

Based on these learning outcomes, the FYS program placed a greater emphasis on forming mentoring relationships and student engagement. The faculty members were assigned as the academic advisors for the students in their course. Each class was also assigned a student peer advisor to help with transition issues. In addition, the first-year students were given the opportunity to select their academic seminar. This process was implemented with the goal of increasing student interest and maintaining their positive attitude toward learning.

Assessment was a critical component of the FYS program. Our assessment package included pre- and post-student surveys, mid- and post-faculty surveys, end-of-semester course evaluations, and a computer-based faculty assessment of learning outcomes. Student surveys focused on perceptions of their experiences in the course, the campus community, and their level of confidence in academic skills. Faculty surveys focused on perceptions of the FYS process, their roles, building student connections, and enhancing academic skills. In addition, the software program eLumen (www.elumen.info) is used university-wide to collect data for assessment purposes. The structure of eLumen requires that its users construct rubrics for each specified achievement of the general learning outcome. Faculty entered data on each student enrolled in their FYS course for each specified achievement. By linking student and faculty surveys with the learning outcomes, we were able to measure student impressions, versus the faculty evaluations to determine whether the FYS objectives were being met. The FYS faculty met in May 2006 to review the assessment results from fall 2005 and used them for course improvement.

This initiative was a faculty-driven program where funding was provided by the College of Arts and Sciences. The director of the first-year seminar wrote a faculty development grant funded by the Bush Foundation to help support the mentoring portion of the program. Grant monies were used to fund the summer meeting of all FYS faculty, mentoring activities, and research expenses. The program was also supported by the Office of Student Services. They provide seminars on study skills, healthy living, and financial decision making as well as tutoring and services for individuals with disabilities. First-year students entering Concordia University with less than 20 college credits or earned college credits occurring as a high school student are required to enroll in the first-year seminar.

Research Design

The program initiative linked assessment tools and learning outcomes to accurately measure whether the students met the objectives of the FYS program. The assessment process provides information for the following question: To what extent does participation in FYS program enhance student engagement with faculty and staff, enhance student's academic skills, and affect student success and retention? A strength of this research design was assessing both student and faculty perceptions on a number of dimensions. Pre- and post-student surveys were developed and implemented at the beginning and end of the first semester. As a wireless laptop campus, the student surveys were administered online. Questions included student perceptions of the FYS common learning outcomes, levels of confidence in their academic skills, and satisfaction with the institution and FYS course. Faculty surveys were distributed at mid-semester and at the end of the term to evaluate their confidence in mentoring roles, their engagement in the FYS program, and the effectiveness of the program and learning outcomes.

Learning outcomes were developed by the entire FYS faculty. A rubric was developed for each specified achievement of the general learning outcomes and entered into eLumen. The rubric scoring structure used the levels of below expectations, meets expectations, and exceeds expectations.

Faculty entered individual student scores for each of the specified achievements. The software package provided automatic feedback and constant updates as data was entered.

Statistical analysis was completed on the student survey data. Pre-and postsurveys were matched to determine if significant differences occurred on the various dimensions assessed during the semester. In addition, analysis was completed comparing the responses from men and women on both the pre-and postsurveys. By comparing this analysis with the faculty evaluation of the learning outcomes, changes were made to improve the program.

It should be emphasized that the learning outcomes are a critical component of the student surveys, faculty surveys, and eLumen assessment. Including survey questions specifically related to the learning outcomes strengthened the design. Comprehensive feedback from multiple sources was essential for effectively evaluating whether the learning outcomes of the first-year seminar program were being met.

Findings

During the 2005-2006 academic year, students completed the presurvey the first week of September and the postsurvey the first week of December. Out of the 165 first-year students, 134 (81%) took the presurvey and 140 (85%) took the postsurvey. All 12 of the first-year seminar instructors gave feedback through the faculty surveys.

Based on the learning outcome of enhancement of academic skills, the first section of the student survey focused on the assessment of students' level of confidence regarding academic skills. Concordia students, similar to other institutions, come with a high level of confidence in their skills. This may have an influence on the FYS curriculum, as students may not feel the need to work on these academic skills. Therefore, the faculty integrated and reinforced academic skills within their academic seminar. In this first section of the student survey, statistically significant differences were found in two questions for our female student population. When asked, "What is your level of confidence in your ability to organize and use time efficiently?" the women's scores went down from the beginning to the end of the semester. However, their scores increased over the semester when asked their level of confidence regarding their ability to write papers for courses. No significant differences for men were found in pre/post assessment.

The second section of the student survey focused on the level of satisfaction with the institution and first-year experience initiatives. In response to the statement, "First-Year Seminar introduced me to the academic skills needed for success in my college courses," based on a four-point Likert scale (4 = agree and 1 = disagree), students reported an average of 2.62. In response to the statement, "First-Year Seminar helped me adjust to college," students reported an average of 2.56. A significant difference between men and women was found when asked to respond to the statement, "First-Year Seminar helped me to understand the expectations of college courses." Men reported an average of 2.72, and women reported an average of 2.25.

Changes were made in the curriculum for the fall of 2006 due to student feedback and continued overconfidence in their academic skills. Given the time constraints of a one-credit course, the FYS faculty decided to narrow the focus of the academic skills to information literacy. The library staff provided workshops for FYS faculty on integrating information literacy skills into their courses. They developed a FYS student research guide to be incorporated into the course. To further reinforce information literacy skills in the curriculum, a member of the library staff was assigned to each FYS course. The Office of Student Services continues to offer courses to enhance effective college reading skills and college foundational skills for those students with the greatest need. They also provided a FYS Student Services conference in September focusing on adjustment to college and expectations of college coursework. This conference allowed the first-year students a choice of topics to help them succeed in their transition to college. Continued cooperation between the FYS program and student services is essential for the success of our first-year students.

Another component of the assessment process was evaluating student and faculty perceptions of the learning outcome developing new mentoring relationships. The FYS program was originally funded through a grant that focused on the value of mentoring. In response to the statement, "I am interested in developing a mentoring relationship with some of my professors," the student average was 3.44 on a 4-point scale. These results reinforce the program initiative of fostering mentoring relationships between students and faculty. The faculty survey responses included: (a) "I feel successful in my role as a mentor" and (b) "I feel supported in my role as a mentor." This feedback emphasized the need for additional support to enhance student and faculty mentoring relationships. To address these issues, faculty shared their ideas of successful mentoring activities during the May FYS faculty meeting. Faculty development in mentoring will continue to be offered to reach this learning outcome. The eLumen assessment provided additional feedback on the mentoring learning outcome of the FYS course. The faculty assessed both the quantity and quality of the relationships with their students. An assumption was made that if students kept all of the advising appointments with their FYS instructor, then the mentoring relationship could be formed. Thus when faculty completed this rubric, more than 60% of our students scored as exceeding expectations in forming these relationships because they attended all of the appointments. After reviewing the rubrics and the assessment data, changes were made in the process of building a mentoring relationship. A registration worksheet and rubric were developed to encourage the students to take more responsibility in forming the mentoring relationship. This tool was developed to encourage students to take a more active role and reflect on how their faculty advisor can help them achieve academic success at Concordia.

After reviewing the faculty surveys and the eLumen data, it became evident that too many learning outcomes were incorporated in the one-credit course. Based on the assessment data, the faculty met in May 2006 to brainstorm the objectives for the fall 2006 FYS course. The faculty decided to keep the same four learning outcomes based on explore, experience, evaluate, and express. However, the number of specified achievements assessed would be limited to allow for more accurate assessment. The achievements for fall 2006 include student engagement, mentoring, and information literacy. In addition, the assessment data have reinforced the decision to offer an academic seminar with variable content to effectively reach our first-year students.

Conclusions

Many lessons were learned from this program initiative. First, it was determined that specific and measurable achievements need to be consistently developed for the FYS learning outcomes. To effectively evaluate the FYS program, specified achievements needed to incorporate consistent measures and quantifiable words to prevent broad interpretations among faculty. Equally important, when developing specified achievements, it is critical to determine what characteristic is really important for students to demonstrate. When evaluating student learning, faculty members found that the rubric levels were not descriptive enough to evaluate student improvement. Further, the data did not provide enough description to effectively guide the improvement of the course. Therefore, the creation of a developmental model was adopted by the university assessment team with the following levels of achievement: no achievement, beginning, developing, accomplished, and exemplary.

Critical components to our success involved technology, engaged faculty, and supportive administrators. First, the use of eLumen and computer-based surveys allowed for an extensive amount of data to be evaluated efficiently and effectively. It is clear that these assessment results will help to define the needs of the first-year students for the entire university. For example, at a recent campus presentation of the FYS survey results, more than 40% of the full-time faculty attended to find out what was discovered. The faculty members at the institution are clearly interested in student success. Second, the FYS program is successful due to the 12 dedicated faculty who make up the team. Their commitment to faculty development, student assessment, and program enhancement allow the program to meet student needs. FYS faculty are engaged in their course because they teach a subject of interest to them and to the students who chose their topic. The faculty reported 4.22 on a five-point scale that the FYS program was a successful addition to Concordia's program for entering students. Third, the support of the administration and the institution's development office is essential in providing adequate funding and grant opportunities to ensure that first-year students are prepared to succeed.

Many benefits were discovered from linking learning outcomes with assessment tools. From this experience, it is strongly recommended that institutions begin the process of linking outcomes with assessment tools. This recommendation is stressed because mistakes made will only help clarify the essential goals of the first-year experience. By beginning this process, it may become evident that learning outcomes or specified achievements need to be eliminated or modified during the development of a program. Through linking assessment tools to learning outcomes, the FYS faculty learned much about the course, the students involved, and the faculty who invested in it.

Primary Contributor

Kristin Bransford
Associate Professor of Psychology
Concordia University
275 Syndicate Street North
St. Paul, MN 55104 -5494
Phone: 651-641-8721
E-mail: Bransford@csp.edu

Additional Contributor

Robert J. Krueger
Associate Professor of Mathematics
Concordia University

Indiana University-Purdue University Indianapolis

Institution Profile

Indianapolis, IN
Public, Four-Year
Designing and Assessing
First-Year Seminars

Editor's Notes

While first-year seminars have been offered at IUPUI for more than a decade, the faculty and staff determined that higher levels of integration between curricular and cocurricular learning were necessary for students. A deeper partnership was formed between the academic affairs and student affairs units responsible for working with first-year students, as well as representatives from the urban community in which IUPUI resides. Particularly noteworthy is the challenge to engage students on this particular campus, none of whom live on site, and the majority of whom are first-generation college students.

The Institution

Indiana University-Purdue University Indianapolis (IUPUI) is a public, four-year commuter institution located in downtown Indianapolis, Indiana. With more than 29,000 students representing 49 states and 122 countries, IUPUI is the second largest campus in the Indiana University statewide multiple campus system. IUPUI is an urban research and academic health sciences campus, with 22 schools and academic units that grant degrees in more than 200 programs from both Indiana University and Purdue University.

IUPUI enrolls 29,953 students. Of those students, 21,172 are at the undergraduate level, with 2,720 being first-year students. The university has an enrollment of 17,236 full-time students and 12,717 part-time students. IUPUI has a significant adult (age 25 and over) student population represented by 14,277 learners. Fifty-eight percent of IUPUI students are female; 42% are male. Total enrollment for students of color represents almost 15% of the total student population. African American students make up 9.4% of the population, Asian/Pacific Islander students make up 3%, and Hispanic students make up 2%. Finally, 62% of undergraduate students are first-generation, defined as neither mother nor father having completed a college degree.

Description of the Initiative

IUPUI supports a large learning community program, offering more than 100 sections of first-year seminar each year. These courses provide tremendous support for the transition and success of new students to the university. Each first-year seminar is taught by an instructional team consisting of a faculty member, academic advisor, librarian, and student mentor.

Specific learning outcomes have been identified for first-year seminars at IUPUI, including: (a) students will begin to develop a comprehensive perspective on higher education; (b) students will have the opportunity to experience a safe, supportive, and positive university learning experience; (c) students will understand and begin to practice good communication skills appropriate to the academic setting; (d) students will begin the process of understanding critical thinking in the university context; (e) students should understand and apply information technology in support of their academic work; (f) students should begin to develop knowledge of their own abilities, skills, and life demands so that they can develop these more effectively in pursuit of their academic goals; and (g) students should understand their role and make full use of IUPUI resources and services which support their learning and campus connections.

In fall 2003, a key student affairs staff position was introduced to strategically work with and support first-year seminar instructional teams, particularly in advancing the goal of students making use of campus resources and services that support learning and campus connections. This staff position performed a variety of functions to encourage and support the integration of cocurricular engagement into the first-year experience at IUPUI. Cocurricular engagement is described as student involvement both on-campus and in the community. The staff position implemented specific initiatives related to first-year seminars including cocurricular program development, instructional team development and support, a weekly newsletter of campus and community cocurricular happenings, and the development of a new first-year seminar course designed to enhance the civic engagement of students at IUPUI.

First, an expanded calendar of cocurricular activities designed specifically to meet the developmental needs of first-year students was introduced. This calendar provided many opportunities for both on- and off-campus involvement. Additionally, a robust agenda of cultural programming designed to help first-year students explore issues of diversity was offered.

Intentional professional development for first-year seminar instructional team members was offered to educate faculty regarding the important role cocurricular learning plays in first-year student success. Instructional team members were taught how to integrate this learning into their course and appropriate ways to engage students in reflection about this learning. Faculty members also took advantage of individual consultations. Additionally, regular classroom presentations in first-year seminars are given to encourage involvement in student life through student organizations, leadership workshops, community service, and other student activities.

The introduction of an electronic newsletter for all first-year students was a significant development in our enhancement of cocurricular learning in the first-year seminars. This newsletter detailed opportunities for campus involvement as well as engagement in the city. Additionally, weekly study tips, provided by the academic advising center on campus, were included.

A newly developed first-year seminar, Discover Indianapolis, served as a vehicle for community integration and engagement for first-year students. Students in this course learned success strategies for navigating the university while being integrated into the local community through the lens of the city's cultural districts. Specific pedagogical strategies were developed to introduce students to traditional first-year seminar topics while also teaching them about the life and culture of the city, and encouraging active community involvement.

This course was taught by an instructional team and included the following goals: (a) helping students develop skills to succeed at IUPUI; (b) introducing students to the life and resources of Indianapolis; (c) sharing information on campus resources; (d) providing a context for assessing interests, values, and abilities so students can make the most of their time at the university; (e) providing a place for students to establish a support network at the university; (f) introducing students to the Principles of Undergraduate Learning; and (g) enhancing understanding and respect for values and practices of the academic community, including respect for diversity, the open exchange of ideas, collegiality, and academic integrity.

In this course, students participated in Service in the City, a large-scale service learning experience designed to further integrate first-year students in the life of the city, educate them about social issues impacting the local community, and introduce them to leaders within the community. Students also worked in groups to complete a final project that allowed them to demonstrate knowledge they learned about Indianapolis and its cultural districts by employing skills learned in the course.

Student cocurricular engagement is an important factor in student satisfaction, success, and persistence. This is particularly true for first-year students where attempts need to be made to assist students in developing strong institutional connections. This often poses a challenge at commuter institutions where the majority of students do not live on campus. By implementing this initiative, we were attempting to increase the engagement of first-year students, both on-campus and in the surrounding community, in educationally purposeful activities that support their learning.

Research Design

For the newly developed Discover Indianapolis first-year seminar, an end-of-course survey was administered to specifically assess student civic engagement and course impact. Students evaluated the course's ability to (a) help them gain familiarity with Indianapolis and learn about the art and cultural offerings in the city, (b) impact their future participation in artistic and cultural events in the city, (c) have an impact on their comfort level in the city, and (d) increase their understanding of local social issues.

In addition, students enrolled in first-year seminars as well as nonparticipants were surveyed using the NSSE. Items specifically measuring cocurricular engagement were compared.

Findings

The implementation of these initiatives was found to be very successful in the enhancement of cocurricular student engagement for first-year students at IUPUI. The data support first-year seminar participation having a statistically significant positive impact on specific measures of cocurricular engagement, including participation in a community-based project as part of a class; attendance at an art exhibit, gallery, play, or theatre performance; participation in community service or volunteer work; and hours per week spent in participating in cocurricular activities.

The Discover Indianapolis course was found to be a very successful tool in enhancing community-based, or civic cocurricular engagement. Additionally, the course made strong impact in students' connectedness to the city, as well as their level of comfort and familiarity with the city.

Table 1

Discover Indianapolis, Fall 2005 End-of-Semester Survey Results

Result of the course	Percent who agreed with statement
I am more familiar with Indianapolis.	100%
I learned about the art and culture offerings in Indianapolis.	84%
I am likely to participate in Indianapolis art and cultural offerings in the future.	61%
I feel more comfortable being in Indianapolis.	50%
I better understand social issues impacting Indianapolis.	89%

A definite challenge for many faculty members was finding time to incorporate one more topic into the first-year seminar course, which is already full of important topics for student success. However, once the first-year seminar faculty discovered how enriching the addition of cocurricular learning was to their curriculum, the student affairs staff member could hardly keep up with the demand for classroom presentations on student life topics. This challenge was offset by the creation of a graduate assistant position, financially supported by academic affairs and housed in student affairs, to provide assistance in instructional team development and support.

The success of this initiative stemmed from the collaborative efforts of academic affairs with student affairs to support both in- and out-of-class learning. Specifically, the development of a key staff position in student affairs to work strategically with University College in supporting first-year student learning was critical to the implementation and success of the initiative. First-year seminars at IUPUI are successful in large part due to the strong support provided by the instructional team model, consisting of a faculty member, a librarian, an academic advisor, and a student mentor. Having faculty and other academic support staff who were willing to implement new ideas (e.g., integration of cocurricular activities into the curriculum, shifts in pedagogy, community-based involvement) is critical.

Conclusions

The enhancement of cocurricular student engagement through first-year seminars at IUPUI provides a model from which other universities may benefit. This is particularly true for institutions where first-year experience courses and related programming is coordinated through academic affairs. Being mindful of the importance of cocurricular learning is an essential element in enhancing programs designed to support first-year student success.

The development of the Discover Indianapolis course as a tool to enhance community-based cocurricular involvement is an initiative that could be developed and piloted on other campuses. Additionally, other institutions may benefit from the development of an instructional team model where a campus-wide approach is taken in the support of first-year students.

Primary Contributor

Frank E. Ross
Assistant Vice Chancellor for Student Life and Diversity
Indiana University-Purdue University Indianapolis (IUPUI)
355 North Lansing, AO 1112
Indianapolis, Indiana 46202
Phone: 317-274-8990
E-mail: frross@iupui.edu

Additional Contributor

Scott Evenbeck
Dean of University College
Indiana University-Purdue University Indianapolis (IUPUI)

Wilkes University

Institution Profile

Wilkes Barre, PA
Private, Four-Year
Designing and Assessing
First-Year Seminars

Editors' Notes

A poorly conceived or executed first-year program may not only fail to produce the desired outcomes, but it may also poison a campus culture against the effort. When those involved are committed to the outcomes and enter the re-design with a willingness to learn from the past, the results of the renewed effort can be remarkable. Wilkes University emerged from a less-than-successful experience to a comprehensive effort that is stronger, more effective, complex, and interrelated, as well as supported by an array of campus constituencies.

The Institution

Wilkes University is a comprehensive institution that today serves nearly 4,500 full- and part-time students. The campus is located in Wilkes-Barre, a city of 43,000 in northeastern Pennsylvania. The University confers undergraduate degrees in the arts and sciences and in professional fields that include education, nursing, accounting, business, engineering, computer science, theatre arts, and communications. Wilkes has masters' degree programs in education, creative writing, business, and a pharmacy doctorate. There is strong institutional commitment to maintaining positive and mutually beneficial relationships with both city leaders and the community-at-large. Many Wilkes students participate in service to the community as part of their curricular, cocurricular, and extracurricular experiences.

In 2005-2006, there were 1,968 FTE undergraduates, including 566 first-time, full-time first-year students. The total Wilkes 2005-2006 undergraduate full-time student population comprised of 47% men and 53% women and was predominantly White (93%). Fifty-five percent of the 2005-2006 full-time undergraduate students were residential students, a figure that includes 75% of the first-year student population. More than one third of the first-year students (35%) reported that neither parent attended college. Approximately 14% of first-year undergraduates enter Wilkes with the intent of pursuing a pharmacy doctorate. Wilkes serves a modest undergraduate part-time student body of 220 students, including 17 first-year students.

Description of the Initiative

In October 2003, the provost of Wilkes University issued a faculty committee report defining the Wilkes Undergraduate Experience as "a guided interconnected journey that personalizes each student's engagement with learning based on individual strengths, aptitudes, learning styles, and career goals" and describing Wilkes graduates as "lifelong learners who make a positive difference in their local and world communities." The Undergraduate Experience is a comprehensive program of intentionally interwoven curricular, cocurricular, and extracurricular activities designed to provide a holistic educational experience. These activities are enacted purposefully throughout the undergraduate years by means of a sophisticated system of developmental advising and mentoring. The Wilkes Undergraduate Experience is further supported by a growing program of student and academic support services and academic and non-academic mentoring initiatives. Wilkes University recognizes that first-year experiences are crucial to a successful undergraduate experience and offers a series of academically based courses specifically focused on the unique needs of first-year students. These courses, as an aggregate, constitute the First-Year Foundations (FYF) Program and all first-year students, regardless of major, are required to participate in the program.

A set of general FYF courses with unified course objectives, but widely varying content, is open to most first-year students. In addition to these general topic courses, a limited number of learning communities, comprising an FYF course and a course in the core curriculum, is available to all unconditionally admitted first-year students. A unique FYF course has been designed to meet the needs of and is required for all conditionally admitted students. The Stretch Writing Program, while not a component of the FYF program, supports the FYF program and provides those entering students who demonstrate significantly underdeveloped writing skills with opportunities to extend their first college-level writing experiences beyond the ENG 101 classroom and beyond the first semester of study. While this paper primarily addresses the FYF courses, it should be noted that first-year students benefit from carefully crafted and significant summer orientation programs that are created cooperatively by FYF faculty and University College staff in an effort to integrate student life and academics.

The design of the present FYF program was influenced in large measure by the failure of a one-credit learning and study skills course offered from 1990 to 1993. The program was eliminated after the fall of 1993 with faculty noting that (a) too many students did not take a one-credit course seriously, (b) there was disagreement among faculty teaching the course concerning the purpose of the course, and (c) the course offered little academic rigor. In short, both faculty and students felt that the course represented an empty one-credit requirement that had little, if any, positive effect on student success.

Wilkes faculty redesigned the university core curriculum in 2000, and, in so doing, created the current FYF program. The central strengths of the Wilkes program, which distinguish it from first-year programs at many other universities, include the following: (a) almost all courses are taught by faculty; (b) instructors may teach whatever topic of personal interest they wish; (c) the academic rigor is equivalent to a typical three-credit first-year course; (d) continued growth and development of the program is driven and guided by the participating faculty members and informed by quantitative and qualitative data gathered from a variety of sources and offices; and (e) the FYF faculty work closely with both University College staff members and student academic advisors to ensure an integrated system of academic challenges, student and academic support services, and developmental advising processes. It must be emphasized that the current FYF program does not and cannot exist and flourish in a vacuum. It is one component of a comprehensive and holistic undergraduate experience.

The FYF program is the only program at Wilkes University required of all students. The core of the program comprises a flexible and changing set of courses that invite faculty to teach in areas of personal interest while supporting a body of common learning objectives, which were approved by faculty committees. These common learning objectives require that each student in the program

- Identifies and applies the following critical thinking processes to course content: analysis, inference, evaluation, openness (i.e., willingness to listen to and empathize with others), and metacognition (i.e., self-monitoring)
- Demonstrates bibliographic skills to accomplish course assignments
- Reviews learning strategies to improve academic performance

- Participates effectively as a member of a collaborative learning group
- Develops effective written and oral communication skills and the ability to seek out, gather, evaluate, and use information appropriate to a given task[1]

Thus, diversity of subject matter and unity of objectives are ensured. General courses in the FYF program are open to all unconditionally admitted students regardless of major and are not intended to be introductory courses within a specific degree program.

The FYF program now receives significant funds from the Office of the Provost and the University College to support continued growth and development. Supplemental funding for instructional support is available and FYF instructors are supported in their efforts by the FYF program coordinator, the learning community coordinator, and the University College staff.

Professional development played a major role in program improvement. Two-day paid workshops have been held for all FYF faculty each summer and are planned collaboratively by the coordinators, the director of University College, and the provost. These workshops provide opportunities for participants to engage in the free exchange of ideas concerning common course objectives, programmatic assessment, and teaching strategies. In addition, they receive training in technological support (including the WebCT electronic advising portfolio and online support for student writing); discuss how to engage students with common readings and with extracurricular and cocurricular learning opportunities in the FYF program; and consider meaningful and coherent ways to incorporate university and program initiatives into the content and delivery of individual courses in support of student learning and holistic development. In addition to these annual two-day workshops, FYF faculty gather throughout the academic year to share ideas and concerns and to plan for the following academic year.

Professional development funds are made available through departments, colleges, the Faculty Development Committee, and the Office of the Provost for participation in conferences and workshops devoted to the first-year experience and for consultations with experts in the field, which inform the ongoing review and development of the program.

Since the implementation of the redesigned First-Year Foundations program, regular review and revision of the previous year's activities, informed by best practices and by information gathered from Wilkes faculty, staff, and students, have ensured the continuous revitalization and enrichment of the program. It should be stressed that FYF faculty are strongly encouraged to participate in the design of activities, initiatives, and programs and to incorporate these opportunities to connect into their course content and delivery. The recommended-but-not required approach was highly successful. Consequently, the FYF faculty incorporated all or most of the following opportunities, as appropriate to the content of their courses:

- Encouraging or requiring students to investigate and attend cultural events on campus and in the greater community and region
- Designing assignments that require students to communicate with advisors using the electronic advising portfolio
- Refering students to appropriate student and academic support services as the need to do so arises
- Informally monitoring student progress in other classes (e.g., by means of conversation, class discussion, student journals, and other activities)
- Encouraging and providing opportunities for students to reflect upon their choices of major and career
- Encouraging or requiring students to identify their learning styles and practices

- Encouraging or requiring students to become involved in university-sponsored community service projects, design a community service project, and attend a variety of campus events

The summer 2006 faculty development work focused on a review of the common course objectives in preparation for the development of valid and reliable assessment measures. It also investigated writing-to-learn practices and teaching strategies for writing that will inform the writing component of all FYF courses and link orientation activities to fall course expectations.

The 2006 FYF program was expanded and enriched, with the cooperation and collaboration of the Office of Student Affairs, through the inclusion of a common reading experience. Several weeks prior to the 2006 orientation program, all incoming first-year students were sent a copy of Jon Spayde's (1998) essay entitled "Learning in the Key of Life." A set of reading prompts designed by the coordinator for writing across the curriculum accompanied the essay, and students were asked to prepare for orientation by reading the essay and responding to the prompts.

During orientation, all first-year students ($N = 600$) were guided by the coordinator for writing across the curriculum through a brief writing-to-learn exercise, which, in turn, was used to inform small-group discussions focused on the question, "What's an education for?" Upper-level students, including resident assistants, peer mentors, and FYF faculty served as facilitators of these small-group discussions. Following this general orientation session, students met in groups according to their course sections with the FYF instructor and continued discussion of the essay and the purpose of education within the context of the course content. Faculty members return to this essay throughout the semester to inform classroom discussions and more extended writing exercises. We believe this communicates a serious commitment to writing, while providing a wealth of opportunities including a unifying theme for diverse courses, opportunities for continuing student self-reflection and inquiry into the nature, meaning, and value of liberal education, and mentoring by both upper-level students and faculty.

Informed by best practices and a faculty-driven process for continuous review and revision, the current FYF program continues to grow and to provide a diverse body of first-year students with a foundation for future learning, growth, and success. Of particular note are the FYF courses entitled Intelligence Applied, which address the unique needs of students who are admitted to the university with conditions. These courses are carefully designed to emphasize effective study habits and strategies while integrating the common course objectives and academic content into a coherent and meaningful developmental experience. The conditionally admitted students complete assignments with the same degree of academic rigor as students in the other FYF courses but receive consistent individualized attention from University College staff.

Learning communities, consisting of pairs of first-year courses (usually including a FYF) with a common cohort of students, foster social bonding and curricular cohesion in significant ways. There are three types of volunteer learning communities: resident only, mixed commuter and resident, and open enrollment. The formalized Learning Community Program is relatively new, and institutional data relating to retention rates, student success, and student satisfaction are not yet available from the University Office of Institutional Research.

Research Design

Wilkes has used both qualitative and quantitative procedures to assess the FYF program. In fall 2001, Wilkes University was one of 63 institutions to participate in a normative study assessing first-year students. The study was commissioned by the Policy Center for the First Year of College, supported by a grant from the Pew Charitable Trusts. The project was a systematic and comprehensive analysis comparing our students to those in peer institutions ($n = 6$), similar Carnegie Class

(n = 25) and all colleges who participated (n = 63). Peer institutions were identified by similar institutional types and articulated learning outcomes of their respective first-year programs.

Additionally, first-year FYF students and upper-level students responded to the Motivated Strategies for Learning Questionnaire (MSLQ) after fall midterms (Lynch, 2005). The MSLQ is a self-report instrument that has been used extensively in previous research investigating college student motivation and learning strategies (Pintrich, McKeachie, & Smith, 1989). The survey yields scores indicating the extent to which students used these well-known learning strategies: rehearsal, elaboration, organization, peer learning, critical thinking, and seeking help.

Findings

The entire program for conditionally admitted students has been a significant success, and, typically, by the end of sophomore year, the grade point averages of conditionally admitted students are no lower (and are often higher) than their unconditionally admitted peers. More specifically, in the benchmarking study, the Wilkes program was ranked most highly compared to peers in effectiveness, improvement of cognitive abilities, and improved life skills. Comparisons with Carnegie peers and all colleges were also favorable (Table 1).

Table 1
Wilkes University's Ranking on Selected Student Learning Outcomes

Factor	Peers	Carnegie	All
Course effectiveness	1	6	22
Course improved cognitive abilities	2	7	23
Course improved life skills	3	2	9

The results from the MSLQ clearly indicated considerable discrepancies between the learning strategies faculty believe to be important in their courses and the strategies that students report using in the course. Both first-year and upper-level student scores showed that the students believed rehearsal to be more important than do the faculty. Faculty rated elaboration, organization, critical thinking, peer learning, and seeking help as factors of greater importance for success in their courses than did the students. As noted above, implications of this pattern have informed a FYF faculty workshop as well as ongoing informal discussions.

Additional assessments suggest that, despite a downturn in fall retention rates in 2006, FYF courses have contributed to significant increases in retention rates of first-time, full-time first-year students since the implementation of the current program in the fall of 2000. In the two years prior to the implementation of the program, Wilkes reported retention rates of 71.2% (fall 99) and 72.7% (fall 2000). In the fall of 2001, however, the retention rate for first-time, full-time first-year students rose to 74.6%, and, with a single downturn in fall 2006, retention rates have risen steadily to hover around 80%. The reported retention rate for fall 2007 is 79.3%, a rate that is 5.4% above the national average for four-year private colleges and universities and 5.6% above the national average for public and private four-year colleges and universities (ACT, 2007; Wilkes University, 2006). The mean retention rate of 2004 and 2005 first-year students enrolled in learning communities was even higher (83%).

The mean retention rate for conditionally admitted students in 2004 and 2005 was 67%. Furthermore, the number of conditionally admitted students whose GPAs were in good standing from 2001 through 2005 varied from 79% to 88%.

Finally, informal surveys of faculty report strong support for the FYF program. Qualitative interviews provide continued insight into yearly changes. Nevertheless, significant assessment challenges remain. It is difficult to identify clearly and assess growth in shared knowledge when each section is focused on a different topic. Differences in faculty opinion about the most appropriate way to assess writing have slowed progress. Finally, it is very difficult to isolate the outcome effects of a single course within the context of all the other factors that may affect student knowledge, beliefs, and behavior. It is encouraging to note, however, that despite these difficulties, the members of 2006-07 FYF faculty have accepted the challenge to discuss and debate assessment issues and, with the aid and support of a variety of offices and constituencies, to begin to develop an assessment plan for the program.

Conclusion

We have attempted to address several concerns in the FYF program. The problems are well known: isolation and self-absorption during the critical first year, early focus on and specialization within a major, an over-reliance upon university support staff that thwarts intellectual and social development, and a lack of meaningful connections with senior faculty. Although no single curricular plan can work magic, the first-year Undergraduate Experience fosters a common learning experience that emphasizes connecting with peers, becoming more comfortable with faculty, and learning to use and appreciate the wider university community to support intellectual and personal development. Specific learning goals related to common readings, writing, oral presentation, and leadership development are intended to enhance this common experience. These are all the more important because FYF is the only required course throughout the entire undergraduate curriculum. Incorporation of several learning communities into the program enhances opportunities for meaningful dialogue across disciplines, while sets of specialized courses, including those devoted to learning strategies and writing, serve the needs of the at-risk student.

The courses provide a common learning experience that engages faculty as well. High faculty involvement pays off by both integrating students into a wide range of academic interests and providing a professional development forum to improve teaching campus-wide.

One of the challenges we hope to address in the future is how to build mentoring connections between sophomores and FYF students. We plan to do this by involving sophomore students who completed the course as peer mentors to the new students. If successful, this will also provide our first planned involvement with sophomores and will be an important development in our campus-wide effort to assist all students.

Notes

[1]The written communication objective was, and continues to be, supported by the adoption in 2005 of a common writing handbook, which is used in all undergraduate courses, including FYF courses and ENG 101, that include writing as a significant factor in determining course grades.

References

ACT (2007). Retention and persistence to degree tables. Retrieved November 5, 2007, from http://www.act.org/path[policy/reports/retain.html.

Lynch, D. J. (2005, December). Differences between student and faculty perceptions of learning strategies. *Teaching Professor,* p. 4.

Pintrich, P. R., McKeachie, W. J., & Smith, D. (1989). *The Motivated Strategies for Learning Questionnaire*. Ann Arbor: National Center for Research to Improve Postsecondary Teaching and Learning, University of Michigan.

Spayde, Jon (1998, May-June). Learning in the key of life, *Utne Reader, 44*, 9.

Wilkes University (2006 , Fall). *2006-2007 Fact Book*, 17.

Primary Contributor

Ellen R. Flint
Coordinator of the Undergraduate Experience
84 West South Street
Wilkes University
Wilkes Barre, PA 18766
Phone: 570-408-4004
E-mail: ellen.flint@wilkes.edu

Additional Contributor

Douglas J. Lynch
Associate Professor
Wilkes University

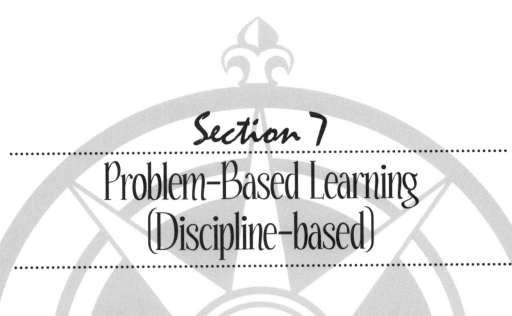

Section 7
Problem-Based Learning
(Discipline-based)

United Arab Emirates University

Institution Profile

Al-Ain, United Arab Emirates
Public, Four-Year
Problem-based Learning
(Discipline-based)

Editors' Notes

The rapid expansion of higher education in the United Arab Emirates (UAE) has been heavily based on Western models. These efforts have often included progressive first-year education models. United Arab Emirates University uses a problem based learning first-year experience. Students, 90% of whom are first-generation college students, tackle issues, across disciplines that have real-world implications for the UAE, such as reducing infant mortality and stewardship of water supplies. Evaluation of the program is both qualitative and quantitative and includes focus groups, classroom observations, and course evaluations by both faculty and students.

The Institution

The United Arab Emirates University (UAEU) is a four-year public institution with an enrollment of approximately 16,000 students. The University General Requirements Unit (UGRU) is the foundation-level program. UGRU consists of over 350 instructors and nearly 6,000 students. The average percentages of women and men in the fall intake over the past five years have been 76% and 24%, respectively, which are comparable to the relative percentages by gender for the entire university population. Approximately 55% of UGRU students are housed in hostels, with the remaining students living in the local community, Al Ain, and commuting to the University on a daily basis. Students entering UAEU come from a wide range of educational backgrounds. The vast majority, nearly 90%, are first-generation university students (Bielenberg, 2005). First-generation students are defined as those whose parents have no college or university experience.

Description of the Initiative

UGRU is a first-year developmental program that aims to foster active, life-long learners who are able to tackle challenging, cross-disciplinary problems. In fall 2003, a set of curriculum competencies were adopted within UGRU. The five competencies are: learner training, thinking skills, application of knowledge, information literacy, and communication. During spring 2004, UGRU sought to identify an engaging means for students to develop the curriculum competencies, and a tool to assess competency levels; the result was the UGRU PBL Experience Course.

Problem-based learning (PBL) is a term coined by Howard Barrows at McMaster University, Canada, in the 1960s. Unlike a traditional project, which is usually designed to consolidate knowledge and demonstrate the relevance of what has already been taught, PBL is inductive in that it begins with the presentation of a real world scenario. This scenario provides the context and motivation for learning. The pure form of PBL designed by Barrows (1992) has been successful in many contexts, but may not be appropriate for all students, particularly those who have come from a didactic, teacher-centered education system that expects students to simply memorize, store, and reproduce information with little opportunity to engage in critical thinking and problem solving. In such cases, students may require additional scaffolding to support their early efforts to work in a group, access and analyze information, and participate in the problem-solving process. When components of more traditional teacher-centered approaches such as mini-lectures and scaffolded guidelines are included in PBL, the process is termed hybrid PBL. It is this methodology that may best serve the needs of the students typically entering the UAE University.

The PBL Experience in UGRU takes place over the period of one 15-week semester for all students in the foundation-year program. Small groups of students (four to five per group) select and work through a real-world problem, applying knowledge and skills gained in other UGRU courses. During the problem-solving process, a facilitator coaches groups on the metacognitive skills of setting goals, recording and monitoring action, reflecting on performance, and assessing progress. The final product includes two recommendations with relevant justification and support in the form of a poster or leaflet. The groups also present their recommendations to the class, usually in the form of a PowerPoint presentation. The key to the whole process is an authentic, engaging real-world problem.

Scenarios. Problem-based learning problems scenarios should be designed in such a way as to ensure that students perform research to gather the information needed for possible solutions (Delisle, 1997). They should be developmentally appropriate, have a clear purpose, have available resources, and be curriculum-based. The topics of scenarios for the UGRU PBL Experience are drawn from student suggestions and the popular press and are guided by the general themes worked on in the English program, such as daily life, work and business, science and nature, sports and leisure, and nutrition and health.

Each semester, students are presented with a choice of three real-world problems that are of current relevance to their lives in the UAE. To date, UGRU students have tackled parking problems, infant mortality, and water resources. A scenario bank includes additional topics such as campus development, traffic accidents, stock market, graduate employment, tourism, library facilities, and sports and leisure facilities. Students indicated a desire to address societal issues such as the increase in divorce rate, and problems around this and other topics are currently being developed.

Task structure. The PBL problem solving process is outlined in Figure 1. Each session begins with students sharing information from their individualized preparation task followed by discussions within the group. Next, personal responsibilities are allocated for the out-of-class preparation task, and each session ends with some form of self- or peer-assessment focusing primarily on the functioning of the group. Each session comes with a clear lesson plan and set of materials for facilitators to use in order to guide students through this process.

Assessment. There is no traditional examination in the UGRU PBL Experience as the students are not expected to acquire subject-specific knowledge. Rather, students develop knowledge, skills, and attitudes in the UGRU Curriculum Competencies that are best assessed using alternative techniques. In addition to a self- or peer-assessment task in each session, there is a standardized teacher assessment component of the work completed for each session, the leaflet or poster created, and group and individual performance on the presentation.

Orientation	• By the end of session, you will understand what PBL is and why we will do it. • By the end of session, you will think about good group work.
Session 1	• By the end of session, you will form groups and choose a role. • By the end of session, you will understand the task and grading. • By the end of session, you will understand a chosen scenario.
Out-of-class	• Before the next session, you will identify what you know and what preparation you need to know.
Session 2	• By the end of session, you will share knowledge and opinions on what you know and what you need to know. • By the end of session, you will write research questions. • By the end of session, you will develop a search plan. • By the end of session, you will share responsibilities.
Out-of-class preparation	• Before the next session, you will find information and take notes.
Session 3	• By the end of session, you will present information to your group. • By the end of session, you will brainstorm possible solutions to the problem. • By the end of session, you will select relevant information. • By the end of session, you will identify gaps in information. • By the end of session, you will make a work plan.
Out-of-class preparation	• Before the next session, you will complete the work plan.
Session 4	• By the end of session, you will share results of individual work. • By the end of session, you will organize information for final product (poster/leaflet). • By the end of session, you will agree to meeting times/responsibilities.
Out-of-class preparation	• Before the next session, you will produce draft poster/leaflet. • Before the next session, you will complete a task sheet.
Session 5	• By the end of session, you will give feedback on other groups' posters/leaflets. • By the end of session, you will plan your presentation.
Out-of-class preparation	• Before the next session, you will finalize your poster/leaflet. • Before the next session, you will practice and assess own groups' presentation.
Session 6	• By the end of session, you will take part in final presentation. • By the end of session, you will write comments on the PBL experience.

Figure 1. The UGRU problem-based learning experience process.

Research Design

Student motivation, curriculum competencies, instructor development, and connections were all assessed using a combination of qualitative and quantitative data gathered through teacher focus groups, classroom observations, and student and teacher course evaluations. The focus groups were held on a bi-weekly basis, with each group consisting of 10 to 15 instructors. Discussions during these sessions were guided by a set of questions distributed to facilitators prior to a given PBL session and completed immediately following the session. Discussion notes were compiled and key themes identified across sessions through careful analysis of the focus group discourse.

Course evaluation forms were completed by both teachers and students at the end of the course. The student course evaluation form consisted of 19 questions covering four main categories: (a) general issues, (b) course documents, (c) assessment, and (d) curriculum competencies. The teacher course evaluation form paralleled the student form and also contained items in the areas of support and content, resulting in a total of 29 items. Responses to individual items were on a four-point Likert scale. Both evaluation forms included prompts for essay responses. The essay responses were read, key themes identified, and responses coded according to these themes. Student and teacher responses were triangulated through classroom observations.

Findings

Overall, the PBL Experience has been found to motivate and engage students while also providing opportunities for them to develop in most areas of the Curriculum Competencies. Data also indicate that students developed a number of connections that will support their learning throughout their university education and beyond. Each of these assertions is discussed below, with supporting data provided.

When compared with other courses, students rate the PBL Experience as the most useful (Table 1). There are three aspects of the UGRU PBL Experience that could lead students to find it more useful than other courses. First, the focus of the PBL experience is on real world problems that are relevant to students' lives. Second, the methodology employed in the PBL Experience is substantially different from that encountered in other courses, with students having much more ownership over their learning. Third, the PBL Experience focuses on skills and dispositions toward learning that will benefit students throughout university and life. We argue that it is a combination of these three aspects that leads the large percentage of students who rate the PBL Experience as useful. We base this assertion on comparison with, in particular, the UGRU Information and Communication Technology (ICT) and Arabic (Study Skills) courses. The UGRU ICT curriculum is task-based, with students assigned real-world tasks such as processing given information to determine possible means of reducing transportation costs of the university. The difference between the ICT course and the PBL Experience is the means by which students are presented information along with student ownership of the learning process. In the ICT classroom, it is the teacher who sets the agenda and determines what will be learned. In PBL, on the other hand, students are presented a choice of problems and take charge of the learning process, with the instructor serving as a guide.

In the Arabic (Study Skills) course, students are introduced to different learning styles and decision-making processes through a teacher-centered approach. While the content of this course is similar in focus to the learner training, information literacy, and problem-solving skills developed in PBL, the methods for promoting them differ substantially, with the study skills course teaching the skills as opposed to having them developed through practice in the PBL Experience.

Table 1

Perceived Usefulness of Courses in the Foundation Year

Course	Percent who find course useful
English	56%
Mathematics	73%
Information technology (IT)	66%
Arabic (Study Skills)	72%
PBL Experience	92%

Students and teachers indicate that the PBL course strongly contributes to the development of the Curriculum Competencies. Information literacy (learning how to access information) and learner training (learning to work in a group, taking responsibility for one's work, and organizing one's work) were rated most highly by both facilitators and students. Eighty-five percent of facilitators and 89% of students agree or strongly agree that the experience helps students learn how to find the information they need and how to use it. Most facilitators (96%) report that the experience helps students to improve their organization of information. While students often found it difficult to analyze the vast amounts of information they accessed, a majority of those completing the essay responses identified this challenge as a major motivating factor. In other words, when presented with challenges that had an authentic purpose, students rose to the challenge and persisted in their efforts. In many ways this is summed up in the words of one of the PBL facilitators, who wrote, "Students' performance levels were all beyond my expectation and to be more accurate I should say way beyond my expectations." This comment was a dominant theme during facilitator focus groups and is one of the most positive benefits arising from implementation of the PBL Experience in our first-year developmental program. As instructors had opportunities to see students succeed, and students experience success in a challenging endeavor, beliefs from both parties about what is possible rose. Setting high standards and providing students with the scaffolding necessary to reach those high standards is becoming more common in UGRU classroom practice.

The final area of positive impact from PBL is in terms of connections. Analysis of the comments on evaluation forms and classroom discourse indicates that PBL enables students to make connections with other learners, between subjects, to the community, to their future, and with their instructors. The connections to both short-term and long-term learning are evident in comments from students:

"I am very happy about this PBL because I learned many things that will be useful in my life."

"It (PBL) was so good, and this will help me in my faculty [i.e., major] studies."

Conclusion

The evidence presented above provides initial insight into the positive impact this curricular initiative had for Arab students in a foundation-year course. Hybrid PBL methodology is a motivating tool that enables the development, application, and assessment of essential knowledge, skills and dispositions necessary for learning for life. Perhaps most importantly, the UGRU PBL

Experience contributed toward the transformation of the broader learning environment, providing a student-centered approach that engages students in active learning. In working toward this, we learned many lessons. First, is the need to involve students and instructors in the entire process, from the suggestion of scenarios to reflection on the learning process. Second, the learning must be anchored to a larger task that challenges students, with the necessary scaffolding provided to aid students in reaching high standards. As such, it is vital that appropriate and available resources be identified for all scenarios ahead of implementation. Students can easily become frustrated if too little or too much information is available to address a given problem. Third, academic language needs should be an ongoing aspect of discussions, particularly when a large number of students have English as a second or additional language, as is the case in the UAE. A final key to the success of PBL in the first-year experience is the incorporation of explicit opportunities for students and facilitators to reflect on group work.

The role of the instructor (facilitator in PBL) is substantially different from the traditional teacher role in a content area class. This change in instructor role can be frustrating for both students and teachers, especially in the initial stages of problem-based learning. On-going professional development is a critical element for any initiative of this sort. It is not enough to simply introduce the concept of PBL to instructors involved in facilitating PBL-based first-year courses or seminars; instructors need opportunities to work with course developers to identify issues and reflect on practice. In our setting, this includes the widespread sharing of facilitator-developed materials and guidelines.

In order to be successful in the 21st century, universities must graduate students who are prepared to be life-long learners. This challenge necessitates a pedagogical shift from transmitting a body of expected knowledge that is largely memorized, to one that is predominately process oriented. In this case study, we demonstrated that PBL is one methodology that can be effectively used in first-year courses to accomplish this goal. It seems appropriate to end with the words of a student who participated in the first UGRU PBL Experience, "I enjoyed working with the group and feeling that our work is so important that we gave it most of our time and thoughts." When first-year students approach learning with this attitude, the possibilities are endless.

References

Barrows, H. S. (1992). *The tutorial process*. Springfield, IL: Southern Illinois University School of Medicine.

Bielenberg, B. T. (2005). Characteristics of the UAE higher education student, *Proceedings of the 6th Annual UAEU Research Conference*, Retrieved January 8, 2008, from http://sra.uaeu.ac.ae/Conference_6/Proceedings/PDF/UGRU/UGRU_3.pdf

Delisle, R. (1997). *How to use problem-based learning in the classroom*. Alexandria, VA: Association for Supervision and Curriculum Development.

Primary Contributor

Brian Bielenberg
Professional Development Coordinator
UAE University, Al-Ain
PO Box 17172
U.A.E.

Phone: +971-50-783-2757
E-mail: bbielenberg@uaeu.ac.ae

Additional Contributor

Maxine Gillway
Curriculum Development Coordinator
UAE University, Al-Ain

West Virginia University

Institution Profile

Morgantown, WV
Public, Four-Year
Problem-based Learning
(Discipline-based)

Editors' Notes

Courses in mathematics are traditionally problematic for first-year students and their success. The content of such courses, and the ways of thinking and knowing that they are centered upon, are widely considered essential elements of a liberal arts education. Yet, too often, there are high rates of failure in these courses. Changing an entire discipline's and department's approach to pedagogy is a daunting task. Yet, the West Virginia University's experience is evidence that it can be done when that change is centered within the faculty and when many work together toward achieving critical goals.

The Institution

West Virginia University (WVU) is located in Morgantown, West Virginia, in the Appalachian Mountains, approximately 70 miles south of Pittsburgh. WVU is an extensive four-year, public doctoral/research university, as classified by the Carnegie Foundation. Enrollment is 26,051 as of fall 2005, with students from all 55 counties in West Virginia, all 50 states, the District of Columbia, and 89 other nations. Fifty-nine percent of the students are state residents, and 41% are nonresidents, with 6,541 graduate and professional students. WVU enrollment is on the rise, with 19,510 FTE undergraduate students, of whom 5,647 are first-year students. All first-year students are required to live on campus. The gender balance is 51% male and 49% female. There are 1,043 students over 25 years of age. The racial/ethnic makeup at WVU is 7% students of color, with 4% African American, 2% Asian, and 1% Hispanic. At WVU, first-generation college students are defined as those whose parents do not have college degrees. The percentage of first-generation college students at WVU is considerable at 25%. WVU ranks nationally in the number of students who have garnered prestigious scholarships, including 25 Rhodes Scholars, 17 Truman Scholars, and 29 Goldwater Scholars.

The Initiative Description

The Institute for Math Learning (IML) was established at WVU in 2000, with the goal to incorporate computer laboratories into the precalculus course. A year of planning and recruiting led to the IML launch and a new instructional computer laboratory. The primary objective of the IML is to reform all courses that are taken before calculus, including Liberal Arts Mathematics, Applied College Algebra, College Algebra, College Trigonometry, Precalculus, and Applied Calculus. Currently, the IML has seven tenured or tenure-track faculty, a visiting assistant professor, six instructors, a lab manager, an administrative assistant, and a computer scientist, along with graduate students and undergraduate lab mentors. First-year and sophomore students are the primary audience for IML courses.

The IML has three core missions (numbers 1-3) and three supporting missions (numbers 4-6):

1. Improve curriculum, instruction, and assessment in classes preceeding calculus through innovative and effective math learning models
2. Provide outreach to K-12 students and teachers
3. Restructure math education courses for K-12 teachers
4. Conduct research to support change in instruction, curriculum development, and assessment
5. Secure grant awards supporting IML initiatives
6. Provide national leadership in innovative and effective math learning models

The IML courses share the following traits:

- All courses include a minimum of eight computer laboratories, which focus on conceptual understanding and application of mathematics.
- The courses measure skill acquisition, conceptual understanding, and problem solving via a variety of assessments including: (a) weekly online WebCT homework quizzes; (b) five online WebCT exams, one of which is a comprehensive final; and (c) conceptual- and application-based labs.
- A goal of the courses is to improve student learning, conceptual understanding, and ability to apply mathematics to solve problems via technology, including: (a) pervasive graphing technology (i.e., applets, software, or graphing calculators); (b) WebCT course management; and (c) Personal Response Systems (PRS).
- The courses emphasize quantitative literacy by demonstrating the utility of mathematics in the students' world.
- The large lectures incorporate active student learning with PRS serving as a delivery mechanism.
- An increase in student accountability is achieved by (a) tracking daily attendance and posting online; (b) class participation as part of attendance; and (c) consistent, frequent feedback on progress via WebCT.
- Instructors report the current grade status for students in WebCT.

In addition to these common elements, IML courses have four general outcomes. First, the courses incorporate multiple representations of mathematical concepts, including algebraic, graphic, and numeric perspectives. Second, the courses focus on communication of ideas, requiring students to explain in written or oral form key mathematical concepts. Third, the courses are built around problem solving, providing opportunities for students to gain experience in analyzing real world problems. Finally, the courses incorporate an element of the history of mathematics so that students can understand mathematics as a human endeavor.

Coordinators in specific IML courses, however, bring their own innovation to implementing the IML components and outcomes. The following highlight specific innovations from each of the courses.

Personal Response System. Liberal Arts Mathematics (Math 121) is typically taken by students in non-science disciplines. Currently, the topics covered include set theory, logic, number theory, geometry, probability, and statistics. One general goal of the course is to stress to these students, who are often disinterested in math, the utility of mathematics in everyday life. Another goal is the development of basic quantitative literacy. In Liberal Arts Math there are typically two to four

PRS questions posed per class, creating a dynamic component to the usually passive activity of listening to a lecture. Students respond to an interactive PowerPoint question using a hand-held input device, then formative data is displayed live to promote class discussion.

Mathematical Modeling. Applied College Algebra (Math 124) has restructured the course from skills development to modeling real-world problems. Learning mathematics in context provides a motivation for students to engage in the course. Poor student preparation in mathematics can be overcome if students view the subject as having utility. So students examine real world data and determine a function model that allows them to make future predictions. They are engaged in using the model to answer questions, motivating the need to solve equations, interpret graphs, and read tables.

Study Guide. College Algebra (Math 126) has as specific goals stressing an algebraic, graphic, and numeric approach to functions, graphing, and equations. One course component that is currently unique to College Algebra is a study guide. The study guide helps students follow the lecture by leaving spaces for them to complete problems that have already been done and blanks for students to complete definitions. The study guide is especially useful for students with learning disabilities.

Collaborative Laboratories. Precalculus (Math 129) combines College Algebra and College Trigonometry for better-prepared students. The laboratory assignments, done in pairs or triads, engage students in activities and are technology intensive. The activities emphasize writing, collaboration, and discourse. In addition to earning points for showing evidence of understanding and doing mathematics, up to 10% of the points are awarded for the ability to work collaboratively, communicate about mathematics in a clear manner, and follow directions and a schedule.

Software Tools. Applied Calculus (Math 150) stresses modeling techniques used in solving real world problems. Its laboratories incorporate Excel worksheets among other interactive tools, providing the College of Business and Economics students' exposure to a software tool used in future classes.

Research Design

Within the IML, all courses have adopted laboratory activities and online assessments as part of the revised course curriculum for first-year students. The impetus for this change has been a need to improve student success in these courses, and the baseline measure for the success of these efforts has been to monitor student grades. Students who receive an A, B, or C are considered to have succeeded in the course. The remaining grades of D, F, and withdrawal are aggregated for each course (called the DFW rate), and the resulting statistics are analyzed for changes in distribution and correlation with any underlying changes in a course's curriculum. To ensure course quality is maintained, success in subsequent courses is also measured. For example, a student taking College Algebra often goes on to take College Trigonometry, so student performance in this subsequent course is tracked as well. Success in a subsequent course is also defined as earning an A, B, or C.

Several courses have implemented other assessments, more specifically, measuring the effectiveness of various curricular changes. An applied college algebra research project is studying the effect of the course on students' ability in and attitudes towards mathematics, as well as the effect of Supplemental Instruction on student success. Supplemental Instruction provides students with an additional day of instruction with a focus on skill development. A retired math ACT test is given as a pre- and posttest to measure cognitive change. A Likert-scale attitude survey is given as a pre- and postassessment to measure change.

In addition to considering DFW rates, the College Algebra and Precalculus co-coordinators have studied the effects of the course restructuring more carefully through several research studies. Since fall 2004, College Algebra students have taken a retired version of the math ACT test.

Precalculus students started taking the test in spring 2006. The math ACT test, used as both a pre- and posttest, is considered an established instrument to measure change in student scores.

The Applied Calculus course has been studying the effects of stratified assessments, which offer students with a wider variety of learning styles an opportunity to demonstrate their knowledge and understanding of calculus. These assessments include individualized semester and gateway exams, online homework quizzes, and group laboratory activities. Students are offered multiple attempts on quizzes and gateways in order to decrease the impact of test anxiety on their performance.

In addition to analyzing student performance on assessments, several other research studies are being conducted. For example, various surveys have been given out in Liberal Arts Math, College Algebra, and Precalculus. Research into PRS use in Liberal Arts Math, College Algebra, Trigonometry, and Precalculus, including course comparisons and survey data is also being conducted.

The Findings

Preliminary findings, based on research currently being conducted, indicate that the IML at West Virginia University is having a positive impact. Before the creation of the IML, the DFW rates in the courses served were as high as 70%. The long-term goal of the IML is to hold DFW rates below 30%. For the 2004-2005 academic year, the Liberal Arts Math, Trigonometry, Precalculus, and Applied Calculus courses held DFW rates at an average 37%, while the Applied College Algebra and College Algebra courses held the DFW rates at an average of 44%. Success in subsequent courses after completing the IML courses has been exceptional, with success rates averaging 80% for those receiving an A or B in an IML course, and 50% for those receiving a C.

ACT scores are currently used to place students into appropriate mathematics courses at WVU. One interesting finding is that students in Applied College Algebra, College Algebra, and Precalculus are not achieving the required ACT score to enter the course. For example, the required score to be placed into Precalculus is 24, while the average pre-test score is 23. This fact highlights one difficulty facing the IML—a lack of student preparedness. However, comparisons of pre- and post-test scores show a statistically significant gain in ACT scores for students in Applied College Algebra and College Algebra. Data from Precalculus will be available next year.

Preliminary data also show that use of a personal response system is having a positive effect. For example, the course coordinator taught two sections of Trigonometry in the fall 2005 semester, one using PRS and one not. The average number of recorded days absent in the non-PRS section was 6.24, while in the PRS section it was 5.50. The DFW rate in the PRS section was 3.8% lower than in the non-PRS section. Further analysis is needed to determine if these differences are statistically significant.

Liberal Arts Math is currently the only IML course without a weekly meeting in the computer lab. Instead, students complete lab assignments on their own. Survey data indicate that students in Liberal Arts Math react less positively to the laboratory component and have a difficult time connecting the material covered in lecture with the topics on the labs. These data suggest that a weekly meeting, in which students can ask questions and receive help when completing labs, is an essential element in the success of IML courses.

Based on the experiences of IML faculty members, support from the provost, dean, and department chair in the implementation of significant course changes is a prerequisite for success. In addition, it is important to realize that coordination of these courses uses an immense amount of time. In order to enhance the effort by faculty on curricular change, the IML plans to implement a system, starting in the fall 2006 semester, in which each course will have a lead instructor. It will be the job of the lead instructor to handle general course coordination tasks (e.g., tracking attendance, posting grades, uploading and downloading spreadsheets), freeing faculty members to focus more on development and improvement of the courses.

Recommendations

In these days of limited resources, competition, and striving for efficiency, many schools seek economy of scale by enlarging section sizes. The IML has achieved success in this environment, but with a significant commitment of the upper administration as shown by (a) investment in laboratory resources, including space, equipment, and staff; (b) promotion of educational technology to make the classroom an active learning environment; and (c) hiring directed toward new faculty predisposed to bring energy and enthusiasm to scholarly work connected with the teaching aspect of the department's mission and faculty evaluation policies designed to encourage and value such work by all faculty.

The best argument to make for this approach is that everyone benefits. The administration gets consistency, improved student success, and engaged instructors. Instructors share experience, course management duties, and structure such as common syllabi and testing. Finally, students have classroom and laboratory activities to provide a varied instructional environment.

Primary Contributor

Robert Mayes
Director of the Science and Mathematics Teaching Center
University of Wyoming SMTC
1000 E. University Avenue
Laramie, WY 82071
Phone: 307-766-5521
E-mail: rmayes2@uwyo.edu

Additional Contributors

Fredrick Butler
Assistant Professor of Mathematics
West Virginia University

Melanie Butler
Assistant Professor of Mathematics
West Virginia University

Edgar Fuller
Assistant Professor of Mathematics
West Virginia University

Michael Mays
Director of the Institute for Math Learning
West Virginia University

Laura Pyzdrowski
Associate Professor of Mathematics Education
West Virginia University

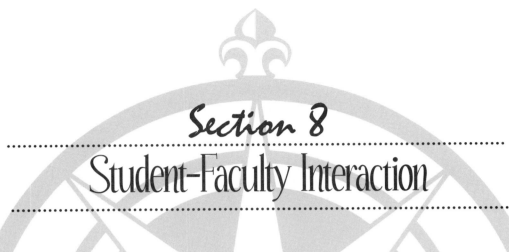

Section 8
Student-Faculty Interaction

Gallaudet University

Institution Profile

Washington, DC
Public, Four-Year
Student-Faculty
Interaction

Editors' Notes

Meaningful interactions between students and faculty have long been considered a contributing factor toward a positive educational environment. These encounters occur intentionally in the classroom but tend to happen more casually outside the formal academic setting. Gallaudet University has taken a purposeful approach to encouraging deeper connections between faculty and students through activities designed to relate typically casual social events with strategic learning and developmental outcomes. Critical to the process is an assessment component that provides evidence of increased student engagement with the institution.

The Institution

Gallaudet University in Washington, D.C., is the world's only liberal arts university for deaf and hard of hearing students. Founded in 1864 by an Act of Congress, its charter was signed by President Abraham Lincoln. Enrollment is approximately 2,000 undergraduate and graduate students. Approximately 35% of the student population is from diverse racial and ethnic backgrounds, including 12% African American, 9% Hispanic, 6% Asian, and 2% Native American. An additional 6% of the students are international. Fifty-three percent of the students are female. Approximately 15% of the entering class is non-traditional. Deaf and hard of hearing undergraduate students choose from more than 40 majors leading to a Bachelor of Arts or a Bachelor of Science degree. The Graduate School offers master's- and doctoral-level programs. The campus also houses the Laurent Clerc National Deaf Education Center, which includes Kendall Demonstration Elementary School and the Model Secondary School for the Deaf.

Description of the Initiative

Based on results of the 2004 First-Year Initiative Assessment, we considered activities to enhance faculty-student connections and out-of-class engagement. We wanted faculty and students in first-year seminar classes to participate in intentionally designed, meaningful activities that promoted connection and out-of-class engagement. We designed a plan to have a series of Movie Nights and opportunities where faculty and students could have meals together. These events were open to all students and instructors in First-Year Seminar (FYS). In some sections, instructors purposefully built Movie Nights into the curriculum. Other instructors met with students often to have meals, while others occasionally did so.

Movie Nights

Two years ago, the First Year Experience program began offering Movie Nights several times throughout the semester to encourage faculty-student connections outside the classroom. Instructors who teach FYS, and their colleagues who teach courses linked to FYS, invited all first-year students to dinner in the cafeteria, followed by a movie and discussion. Instructors chose movies related to topics addressed in their classes, including *The Lost Boys of Sudan* (i.e., culture shock, identity, peer support) and *Tuesdays with Morrie* (i.e., teacher-student relationships). Discussions after the movies have included graduate students from related departments as well as other interested faculty and staff members. Other films we have shown include *The Boys of Baraka*, *Whale Rider*, *Bend It Like Beckham*, *Dead Poets Society*, and *Partners of the Heart*.

Lunch (Breakfast and Dinner, Too) with Students

The First Year Experience program has also worked with our food service administrators to offer FYS instructors free meals in the cafeteria any time instructors choose to eat with their students. Since the program's inception in 2004, during each semester, FYS instructors (and faculty or staff members who give presentations to classes) have regularly taken advantage of this program. Sharing meals with students takes other forms at Gallaudet as well. For the past few years, several FYS instructors have cooked for their classes, either at Thanksgiving or during the last week of the semester. Several instructors have taken their classes to restaurants, using stipends from the First Year Experience program. For example, one Korean faculty member took his students to a Korean restaurant to share his culture.

Research Design

At the end of each semester, the First Year Seminar (FYS) course is assessed using the EBI First-Year Initiative (FYI). The EBI FYI is a commercially designed tool that measures the effectiveness of the FYS course by providing benchmarking data. Institutions can compare themselves to like institutions, all institutions that participate, and they can also look at change over time within their own institution. Students respond to questions about whether or not they believe the course has positively impacted them in a variety of areas. Two areas of student engagement were of interest, and therefore, research questions were posed: As a result of the Movie Night program and meals with students, would out-of-class engagement and connections with faculty as measured by the FYI increase? In addition, would there be differences in these factors in sections of FYS where students were required to attend such events, or in sections where students reported having meals with faculty? Baseline data from 2004 EBI First-Year Initiative were compared with 2005 results.

Findings

Results of the EBI First-Year Initiative indicate statistically significant differences between students' responses to questions about out-of-class engagement and connections with faculty for academic years 2004 and 2005. In addition, section analysis indicated that in classes where faculty required or strongly encouraged attendance at Movie Nights or where students reported either attending one Movie Night or sharing at least one meal with a faculty member, responses on these two factors were higher than the Gallaudet mean (Table 1).

Table 1

Gallaudet FYI Assessment 2004 and 2005

	2004 (N = 207)		2005 (N = 152)	
	Mean	**Std. Dev.**	**Mean**	**Std. Dev.**
Increased out-of-class engagement	4.21	1.89	4.60	1.82
Increased connections with faculty	4.97	1.58	5.33	1.82

Note. Comparisons based on 2005 EBI First-Year Initiative Study.
$p < .05$

Student Narrative

Students reported through course evaluations that their experiences with Movie Nights were helpful in providing diverse perspectives on issues and valuable in enhancing the faculty-student relationship. In their reflective journals, students, who attended *Tuesdays with Morrie*, expressed their appreciation for the discussion with the social work graduate students. It was their first experience participating in a discussion with graduate students, and several of the first-year students reported feeling proud of their ability to engage in such discourse.

Two honors-level First Year Seminar classes attended a graduate-level counseling class on death and dying to view and discuss the series of *Nightline* interviews with Morrie Schwartz. Students' journal entries again expressed pride in their discourse. During a break in the graduate class, the honors students asked extensive questions about the counseling field, and several reported an interest in exploring the field further.

Although they were open to all FYS classes, the showings of *The Lost Boys of Sudan* were specifically intended for students in First-Year Seminar/biology linked classes. Students reported that these discussions, which included faculty members and graduate students in social work as well as the FYS students, were both lively and inclusive, helping the new students to feel welcomed in an academic event. Comments from students' journals included the following:

> I appreciated the discussion after 'The Lost Boys,' because I learned from all of the many questions that came up. From now on, I have to read more world news and research events on the Internet. I realize now that many Sudanese are dying every day and the world doesn't pay attention.

> 'Dead Poets Society' connects to our class on different levels. When we discussed conformity, we had a real variety of perspectives on college life and fitting in. And the movie really opened our minds about how different teachers look at learning and power in the classroom.

> 'The Boys from Baraka' really touched our hearts. I could see that when I saw so many students crying at the end of the movie. We saw those boys change their lives for the better, and we saw that we could do that, too.

Students reported in course evaluations and their reflective journals that they felt the experience of sharing meals with their instructors enhanced their relationships. Instructors' reports were enthusiastic, often expressing their appreciation for the opportunity to interact with their students in an informal setting.

Faculty reported that when sharing meals with students, while often planned around class activities, questions regarding a wide range of campus issues and concerns were raised. These naturally occurring conversations among faculty and students were often the highlight of the time together.

Conclusions

Based on the results of the EBI First-Year Initiative (FYI) and student narratives, it appears that creating intentional opportunities for students to interact with faculty helped to increase students' connections with them as well as out-of-class engagement.

Some of the questions that make up the factors may not be directly impacted by Movie Nights and meals with faculty (i.e., course improved understanding of faculty expectations of students or feedback from students); however, all questions in each factor improved from 2004 to 2005 and were higher in class sections where Movie Nights were required or meals were shared. It is most likely that when students interact more often with faculty, many aspects of faculty-student engagement are naturally enhanced.

The costs for such initiatives are small in comparison to the significant gain in student-faculty and out-of-class engagement. While relatively simple and inexpensive to initiate, the effect on first-year student engagement is substantial. From our experience, we offer the following suggestions to FYE programs considering their own Movie Night program or lunch and dinner with faculty:

1. Choose films that clearly connect to your curriculum, and make those connections explicit to students.
2. Involve students, student affairs professionals, and faculty in the selection process.
3. Invite faculty and staff from relevant programs to lead discussions and extend invitations to students majoring in their academic program.
4. Remember that food attracts students. Whether it is snacks with a movie or a meal, feature food in your publicity.

Primary Contributor:

Catherine Andersen
Interim Dean, Enrollment Management and General Studies
Gallaudet University
800 Florida Ave N.E.
Washington, D.C. 20002
Phone: 202-651-5804
E-mail: catherine.andersen@gallaudet.edu

Additional Contributors

Judith Termini
Interim Director of the First-Year Experience (FYE)
Gallaudet University

Maria Waters
FYE Program Coordinator
Gallaudet University

University of Georgia

Institution Profile

Athens, GA
Public, Four-Year
Student-Faculty
Interaction

Editors' Notes

Learning communities are particularly and increasingly important to first-year success at large universities, where they provide a context for making the "large institution small." The stakes for success are particularly high at the University of Georgia, where underperformance in the first year can mean loss of the Hope Scholarship. In a program that is expanding, UGA's learning communities have taken in students whose academic profile and predictions are below those of their fellow students. The learning community students, however, have outperformed their non-community peers, and the program continues to evolve through multiple sources of program evaluation.

The Institution

The University of Georgia (chartered in 1785), located in Athens, Georgia, is a four-year, public, Research I institution and also the state's land-grant and sea-grant institution. The university is primarily a residential campus, with a new regulation requiring all first-year students to live on campus. In fall 2005, the University of Georgia (UGA) enrolled a total of 33,680 students, of which 25,204 were undergraduates and 4,711 were first-year students. Students come from all 50 states as well as Washington, D.C., Puerto Rico, the Virgin Islands, and 128 different countries. The majority of undergraduate students, however, are from the state of Georgia (21,489 out of 25,204). The counties of northeast Georgia, particularly the Atlanta area, provide an ever-increasing percentage of our students.

For fall 2006, the UGA Factbook listed the undergraduate population as 40% male, 60% female. Racial and ethnic groups represented within the undergraduate population include: White (81.0%), Asian/Pacific Islander (5.6%), Black/African American (5.3%), multiracial (2.3%), Hispanic (2.0%), American Indian (1.1 %), and not reported (3.7%). The entering class of 2006 included 383 students for whom at least one parent did not graduate from college (i.e., complete a bachelor's degree).

Description of the Initiative

The University of Georgia Learning Communities Program, established in 2004-2005, began with a committee appointed by the vice president for instruction. The committee included representatives from his office, housing, admissions, and the registrar, together with associate deans and faculty from the Franklin College of Arts and Sciences and the Colleges of Education and Social Work. The program focuses entirely on entering students who are beginning their first semester at the university; transfer students are not included. The students are typically 18 years old. Members of the learning communities are self-selected. Though the numbers vary from year to year, overall the SAT scores and predicted GPA of LC members are slightly lower than those of the average UGA first-year student. The LCs generally have greater racial and ethnic diversity than the entering class, and involve significantly fewer honors students than the entering class as a whole (3.5% for LC classes entering in 2004 and 2005, as opposed to 10% of the first-year population). Principal goals for the project included enhancing the students' learning environment and providing a sense of intimacy within a large university setting.

In the UGA Learning Communities (LCs), students are organized into cohorts of 20 students focusing on a common academic discipline or theme. They live together by gender on the same floor of a single high-rise residence hall. Learning community students take three classes in common: (a) a core-requirement class linked to the chosen topic, usually in a large lecture format (three credit hours); (b) a first-year composition class (three credit hours); and (c) a first-year seminar with a "lead instructor" (one credit hour), a senior faculty member who integrates the academic aspects of the community and supervises the students' participation in service-learning projects during the spring semester. In fall 2004, we began with four learning communities: Education, International, Science, and Social Sciences. Student enrollment was 71. In the fall 2005, there were five learning communities, entitled Global Engagement, Life Sciences, Literature on Stage, Music, and Social Sciences; student enrollment was 90. Fall 2006 featured eight learning communities: The Art Experience, Business, Life Sciences A (cell biology emphasis), Life Sciences B (environmental emphasis), Global Engagement, Music, Literature on Stage, and Pre-Law; total enrollment was 155 students.

In this case study, we chose to focus particularly on the Life Sciences and Social Sciences communities because the instructors had worked together over a two-year period, while in other communities instructors changed annually. In addition, the instructors of these two communities collaborated intensively and worked intentionally to integrate writing with the learning of subject matter.

The life sciences learning community followed a model in which the first-year seminar instructor (i.e., lead instructor) collaborated with the composition instructor. Students in the first-year seminar course attended research lectures in the Department of Cellular Biology, then filled out a response form after each session and discussed the experience with the lead instructor in the next class meeting of the first-year seminar. In writing assignments, students also described four of the research sessions for a non-specialist reader, their first-year composition instructor. The composition class also emphasized writing within the discipline and involved a research project modeled on scientific writing genres, which included writing the methodology, a literature review with annotated bibliography, and a research paper with accompanying abstract.

The social sciences learning community followed a model of collaboration between the core content and composition faculty. The sociology and composition instructors shared syllabi and used one film in common. While there was no explicit collaboration, the composition instructor encouraged students to incorporate information and concepts from their sociology class into composition class discussions and essays, using the content-area course as a support for writing instruction while increasing students' understanding and knowledge of the discipline. The social sciences LC also emphasized writing for an audience and learning the genres of disciplinary discourse.

Research Design

Given the program's profile and the fact that it is in the early stages of development, we were concerned first of all with measures of basic achievement at the end of the calendar year, in particular, the relation of actual GPA to predicted GPA and retention of the HOPE scholarship.[1] We were also interested in students' reflections on less quantifiable benefits of the experience. Finally, we were interested in how the combination of a composition class with a disciplinary class, the hallmark of UGA learning communities, would impact student performance.

First, we compared predicted and actual GPA at the end of spring semester of the students' first year. For learning community students, data for individual predicted GPAs are provided by the Office of Admissions for assessment purposes on a strictly confidential basis. We also compared the performance in the large content-classes by LC and non-LC students. Various qualitative methods were also used to assess the impact of the program, including awards and recognition granted to the learning community students and programs, in addition to student reflections on the program. Finally, in 2005-2006, we also examined student reflections about the learning communities gathered by the composition instructors.

Beyond this study, graduate students in the Department of Counseling and Human Development Services are annually conducting additional assessment of the impacts of the learning community program. A web-based survey instrument is used to evaluate student experiences in areas such as transition to college, academic involvement, and community engagement. The assessment follows a pre- and post-experience design, with surveys conducted early in the fall and late in the spring semesters. Learning community students are compared to a similar, non-learning community cohort from a companion first-year residence hall. Additional detail subsequently is gathered from interviews with select focus groups.

Findings

As first-year students, members of the learning communities generally exceeded their predicted level of achievement. In both 2004-2005 and 2005-2006, LC students performed well in relation to the general measures of success, with more than 63% exceeding their predicted GPA. For students entering in fall 2004, admission predictions for GPA were actually slightly higher than the entering class as a whole (3.19, as compared with 3.15). What is significant, however, is that while the actual cumulative GPA for the first-year class as a whole matched the admissions prediction precisely, the actual cumulative GPA for the learning communities was 3.35, or 0.16 points above their predicted average, with one third of the students improving their predicted GPA by more than 0.25 points. In terms of HOPE scholarship retention, 83% of the students in the 2004 cohort attained a GPA that would enable them to retain the scholarship. For students entering in fall 2005, the predicted GPA was slightly lower than the entering class as a whole (3.26, as compared with 3.28). The actual average cumulative GPA for all students was lower than predicted, with both the learning community students and the first-year class as a whole earning 3.18. What is significant is that over half of the learning community students, 63%, exceeded their predicted cumulative GPA by spring 2006; 66% attained the 3.0 grade-point average necessary to retain the HOPE scholarship, and 33% exceeded their predicted average by more than 0.25 points.

Qualitative data further supported this assessment that students in the learning communities performed better than expected. Learning community students have an unusually high representation in the Honors Day recognition ceremonies held at the University of Georgia each spring. While only 4% of the 2004 cohort and 3% of the 2005 cohort of the learning communities were also honors students as incoming first-year students, 13% of the learning community first-year students each year were recognized as being in the top 5% of their class. Furthermore, in 2006, some members of the 2004 cohort were honored again, with 8% maintaining their status in the top 5% for the second year. Two learning community students also earned the Barnett Award for outstanding essays written in first-year composition courses from the English Department.

Students in the learning communities also earned higher grades in the large-lecture content classes than their peers who were not in a learning community. For all sections in the first two years of the program, in the content class learning community students scored higher than non-learning community students by an average of 0.21 GPA units ($n = 11$ classes with total LC and non-LC enrollments of > 200 and > 300, respectively).

Data from the 2005-2006 LCs emphasized in this study (life sciences and social sciences), offer further evidence that students in the learning communities performed better in the large lecture class than did their counterparts who were not in the learning communities. In Sociology 1101, students in the social sciences LC earned far more A and B grades and far fewer Cs than did the class population as a whole (41% of learning community students earning As, as compared to only 16% for the non-LC students, with a total of 88% earning As or Bs, as compared with 72%). The average course grade for the learning community students was 88%, as opposed to 82% for the non-LC students, or a group GPA of 3.29 for LC students and 2.82 for non-LC students. This gap is particularly significant in terms of HOPE scholarship retention.

Likewise, in the core Chemistry 1211 class, students in the life sciences learning community earned significantly more A and B grades than the non-LC students (72%, as compared to 57%, with 36% of the learning community students earning As, compared to 23% of non-LC students; the overall group GPA was 2.44 for the learning community students, as compared to 2.31 for non-LC students). Furthermore, in the Chemistry 1211 Lab, the LC students earned significantly more As than the non-LC students (44% as compared to 32%).

Additional data from 2005-2006 suggest that students in the learning communities demonstrated better academic work habits in their large lecture course than did non-LC students). For instance, students in the social sciences LC missed fewer discussion sections than did the non-LC students (0.3 as opposed to 2 classes per semester). Life sciences LC students also had a significantly lower drop rate in chemistry (two out of 19 students as opposed to the general withdrawal rate of 23%). These statistics suggest that group ethos and sense of community play a significant role in student success.

Concerning the performance of learning communities in First-Year Composition, the evidence is less conclusive. The capstone project for FYC is a portfolio of written work that is graded by two instructors. The learning community students, as a body, received slightly higher grades on their portfolios than did non-LC students, 85.58 as compared with 84.73. Students in the social sciences LC earned an average portfolio score of 85.19, and students in the life sciences LC earned an average portfolio score of 86.00. The aversion of science students in particular to writing and the slightly lower predicted success of LC students within the general UGA population indicate that these results, although not statistically significant, are encouraging.

Clearly, the structure of the UGA learning communities, partnering a disciplinary course with a composition class, and their collaborative ethos improved student performance in their classes. The exact role played by writing-to-learn and disciplinary writing in that success will require further study. Nevertheless, the writing generated by the two cohorts upon which we focused provides evidence of less quantifiable benefits, both academic and social. One student who was frightened of taking chemistry wrote:

> I knew that if I had some of my peers to study with, things would be much different. Now, I will say that I'm not doing extremely well in the course but if it weren't for the help of people in the learning community, I would be doing much worse. . . . I know if it was not for them, I would be looking for another school to transfer to right now. (Student essay, November 2005)

Another found the program's level of diversity crucial to her intellectual and personal development. A White female student who came from a small town in which the Ku Klux Klan had had a strong presence, wrote that while she had "never been taught to be racist," she also had experienced little contact with members of other races. While she had not considered diversity as a factor when joining the learning community, it was there that she developed one of her "closest friendships" with an African American female student. In her personal essay, the young woman describes their friendship in depth, emphasizing all of the tastes and viewpoints they share in common. In contrast, her friend was seeking diversity in the learning communities. At first, she "found it easy" to become close to learning community students who were of Asian, Indian, and Middle Eastern descent, delighted to find that skin color and background did not seem to matter in the community. However, this student also discovered that "different personalities hindered" her ability to form lasting, close friendships with these students. She looked instead to someone who was "the same academically and socially" as herself and was surprised to find that her best friend turned out to be White (Student essay, November 2005). Similar sentiments were echoed by other students.

Conclusion

In 2005-2006, the UGA learning communities received the annual Collaborative Teamwork Award from the Division of Student Affairs. Starting small has allowed the University of Georgia learning communities to create a foundation of stable working relationships that supports an already strong program as it continues to expand.

Notes

[1] The Hope scholarship pays for tuition and books at in-state institutions for all students who are Georgia residents graduating with a high school average of B and who maintains B average in college.

References

HOPE Scholarship. University of Georgia Office of Financial Aid. Retrieved April 26, 2006 from http://www.uga.edu/osfa/hope.html

University of Georgia Fact Book 2005. Office of Institutional Research. Retrieved April 25, 2006 from http://www.uga.edu/irp/factbks.htm

University of Georgia Learning Communities. University of Georgia. Retrieved April 26, 2006 from http://www.uga.edu/learningcommunities/

University of Georgia Learning Communities Advisory Board. University of Georgia. Retrieved August 11, 2006 from http://www.uga.edu/learningcommunities/advisory_board.htm

Primary Contributor

Christy Desmet
Associate Professor of English and Director of First-Year Composition
Department of English, Park Hall
University of Georgia
Athens, GA 30602-6204
Phone: 706-542-2128
E-mail: cdesmet@english.uga.ed

Additional Contributors

Sharon D. McCoy
Instructor of English
University of Georgia

June Griffin
Franklin Fellow
University of Nebraska

Joe W. Crim
Associate Vice President
University of Georgia

Marcus Fechheimer
Josiah Meigs Distinguished Professor of Cellular Biology
University of Georgia

Western Illinois University

Institution Profile

Macomb, IL
Public, Four-Year
8,000
Student-Faculty
Interaction

Editors' Notes

Particular strengths of Western Illinois' first-year program are its anchoring in current coursework, the depth of faculty involvement, the establishment of measurable goals, and the pedagogical standards that are necessary for a course to be designated as a First Year Experience Course. The designated program is relatively young, currently offering some 40 courses in 80 sections and 20 departments, taught by 40 tenured and tenure-track faculty in sections of no more than 20 students. All sections feature interactive learning techniques, out-of-class experiences, and peer mentorship. The depth of the administration's commitment is demonstrated by the naming of an associate provost for undergraduate education.

The Institution

Western Illinois University (WVU) is a public, comprehensive four-year master's granting institution located in Macomb, Illinois, a town with a population of approximately 20,000 in west central Illinois. Within our student population of 13,000, first-year students (approximately 2,000) are required to live on campus in residence halls for their first two years.

Of the 11,284 undergraduate students enrolled in the fall 2005 semester, 51.3% were men. The majority (81.5%) were White students. Other ethnicities reported by students included African American (6.9%), Hispanic (3.8%), Asian American (1.4%), and international (1.1%) with 21.5% of students 25 or older. Data reported by approximately 85% of the 1,816 first-time, first-year students on the Beginning College Survey of Student Engagement indicated that 44.4% are first-generation students, which is defined as having parents or legal guardians who did not complete a four-year college degree.

Description of the Initiative

Our First Year Experience (FYE) courses were piloted in 2004 with approximately 200 honors students participating. The honors students introduced FYE to the campus in a positive light, avoiding the stigma of remediation. Then, in fall 2005, all incoming students who have completed 15 or fewer hours of college coursework were required to enroll in two FYE courses; one each during their first two semesters.

An FYE planning committee, composed of a faculty member majority and multiple representatives from student services, admissions, advising, the registrar's office, college deans, and department chairs, determined that the concrete and measurable goals for the academic course component of FYE are to

- Allow students to develop personal relationships with other incoming students, with one or more traditional faculty members, and with one or more upper-division students
- Expose students to learning experiences outside of traditional classes and to demonstrate how those experiences relate to academic content
- Avoid developing a structure of course offerings which would be difficult to sustain

These goals were in line with our institution's overarching strategic plan and were thought by the committee to be attainable, yet progressive goals.

FYE courses are specially designated sections selected from existing courses in our curriculum. In 2005-2006, the majority of the approximately 200 FYE course sections were selected from our social science and humanities general education course offerings, although about 10% were selected from introduction to major courses (i.e., law enforcement, agriculture, and business). To be chosen to receive the FYE designation, the course needed to be a three- or four-credit hour course offered at the 100 or 200 level. In addition, department chairs were asked to identify tenured or tenure-track faculty to teach FYE courses. We found faculty were attracted to the first-year only sections and capping enrollment at 20 students. The interested faculty tended to work well with newly matriculated students and excelled in class discussion and student engagement. Eighty faculty members taught 40 FYE courses across 20 departments, which represented every college at WIU.

Faculty teaching a FYE section are expected to incorporate at least three activities into their class, to use the services of a peer mentor, and to use interactive pedagogical techniques. Beyond these basic requirements, the content of the class is not expected to be different than the regular (non-FYE) sections offered of the same class.

Cocurricular activities. Faculty are asked to ensure that their students attend at least three out-of-class activities, preferably as a group. Faculty have complete autonomy in choosing which cocurricular events their students will attend, though information is regularly shared with faculty about events that are occurring on campus. Popular choices of cocurricular events during 2005-2006 were concerts, plays, films, speakers, field trips, and social or study sessions. Faculty are expected to integrate the cocurricular components into the class content in some fashion. Typically, faculty integrated these events through class discussions, and/or by asking students to write formal or informal papers incorporating the event.

Peer mentors. Faculty members are expected to choose a peer mentor who is typically an upperclass student either majoring in the discipline or who has taken and excelled in the class in the past. Faculty are allowed a great deal of latitude in determining the duties for their peer mentors. Generally, peer mentors attend the cocurricular events and often lead discussions about them. Many peer mentors choose, or help the professor choose, the cocurricular events. Some peer mentors attend the FYE classes regularly and participate in various ways. Peer mentors receive a small honorarium for serving in the role.

Units involved. FYE courses are administered by the Provost's Office. The position of assistant provost for undergraduate studies was created, in part, to lead implementation of the FYE planning committee recommendations. The assistant provost worked closely with academic and associate deans, the registrar, the director of the University Advising and Academic Support Center, institutional research staff, and faculty governance leaders to initially identify a set of courses for FYE designation. Deans and department chairs then identified faculty members to teach those sections.

The outgoing chair of the Faculty Senate was selected to serve, part time, as a faculty associate for FYE in faculty development. He worked with a group of faculty members, associate deans, student services personnel, and the assistant provost to create a FYE Faculty Workshop to provide guidance to fall 2005 FYE faculty. New FYE faculty for spring 2006 were expected to participate in similar versions of this workshop, and all faculty teaching FYE courses in the future will be asked to participate in an additional workshop. The faculty associate for FYE maintained contact with FYE faculty throughout the year, providing information and advice through electronic media, and hosting workshops and speakers to support FYE courses.

A graduate assistantship was created to support FYE courses as well. The graduate assistant was identified as the peer mentor coordinator, and she maintained contact with all peer mentors through each academic semester. She also conducted focus group assessment sessions with peer mentors, created a training session for peer mentors each semester, and created and hosted a reception to present FYE awards each semester.

While the FYE courses are offered and administered through Academic Affairs, the vice president and staff members in Student Services are involved in coordinating how the FYE courses integrate with the FYE living-learning communities in the residence halls. Housing and dining personnel, orientation and student development personnel, and advising personnel—representing both vice presidential areas—work together to offer orientation and registration programming, which highlights the FYE courses as well as other aspects of the FYE Program at Western Illinois University.

Support. The university president initiated the FYE planning committee and worked with campus constituencies to compose an appropriate membership. The president worked with other top-level administrators to create a substantial budget. Allocated funds for the program from this budget were primarily used to hire new faculty members to teach classes for displaced students seeking general education credit.

Research Design

A primary form of assessment of the first full year of FYE course implementation was survey data from both students and faculty. The first-year students enrolled in FYE courses completed an online survey near the end of both the fall 2005 and spring 2006 semesters. The survey included 61 items focused on WIU values and the stated goals for the FYE program, with particular attention to interpersonal relationships between students and faculty and to students' exposure to out-of-class activities in relation to academic content. Responses to selected items are included in Table 1.

Faculty members who taught FYE courses received online surveys near the end of each semester. Many of the items were similar to the student survey asking for the faculty view of their students' outcomes. Additional items focused on the implementation of the courses. Selected responses are included in Table 2.

Responses were measured using a Likert scale (6 = strongly agree, 1 = strongly disagree) and included a residual category of not applicable. The data reported are condensed percentages of responses to the three "agree" categories.

Table 1

First-Year Student Survey Responses Concerning FYE Courses

| | Fall 2005 | | | Spring 2006 | | |
| | | % of | | | % of | |
	N	agree	mean	*N*	agree	mean
Interpersonal Relationships						
My FYE instructor really cares about me as a person.	528	75.4	4.5	189	75.7	4.6
My peer mentor takes a personal interest in my success at Western.	466	36.1	2.9	174	36.6	2.9
I know my FYE instructor better than I know my other WIU instructors.	545	60.5	4.0	202	57.8	3.7
I feel comfortable talking to my FYE instructor about:						
academic difficulties	547	75.0	4.5	202	79.6	4.6
personal concerns	535	53.1	3.7	196	56.3	3.8
I feel comfortable talking to my peer mentor about:						
academic difficulties	465	41.2	3.1	176	41.9	3.1
personal concerns	465	30.3	2.8	174	39.0	2.8
Western's FYE program has a positive impact on my relationships with:						
faculty members	540	61.8	3.7	202	64.9	3.8
fellow students	543	63.4	3.8	197	65.8	3.8
Western's FYE program enables me to respect the views of others.	550	64.6	3.6	199	67.3	4.0
My FYE course involves more class discussion than my other WIU courses.	550	77.0	4.5	206	74.9	4.3
My FYE instructor encourages class discussion.	553	92.8	5.1	214	94.2	4.9
Out-of-Class Activities						
My FYE instructor regularly makes the class aware of the activities occurring on campus.	552	86.4	4.8	206	82.0	4.6
Western's FYE program encourages me to become involved in campus activities.	550	67.5	3.9	204	71.2	4

Table continued p. 149

Table 1 continued

| | **Fall 2005** | | | **Spring 2006** | | |
	N	% of agree	mean	*N*	% of agree	mean
Western's FYE program helps me appreciate that learning extends beyond the classroom.	545	59.8	3.7	202	61.5	3.7
Out-of-Class Activities I attend non-residence hall, out-of-class activities with my FYE classmates.	546	63.0	3.9	202	74.4	4.3
Participation in out-of-class activities is included as a part of my FYE class grade.	547	86.5	4.9	205	85.0	4.8

Note. Percentage of agree is a combined average of all three agree categories.

Table 2
Faculty Survey Responses Concerning FYE Courses by Faculty

| | **Fall 2005** | | | **Spring 2006** | | |
	N	% of agree	mean	*N*	% of agree	mean
Interpersonal Relationships The small enrollment feature of this FYE class has helped me get to know my students better as individuals.	96	87.6	4.9	73	87.7	4.8
My FYE students in this class feel comfortable talking to me about:						
academic difficulties	94	81.4	4.4	69	86.3	4.0
personal concerns	88	66.0	4.0	69	68.5	4.0
Western's FYE program helps enable students to respect the views of others.	86	74.2	4.2	69	71.2	4.1
This FYE course involves more class discussion than my other WIU courses.	96	70.1	4.21	73	72.6	4.3
Having a small enrollment promoted positive faculty-student interaction in this FYE class.	97	90.7	4.8	73	89.1	4.8

Table 2 continued p. 150

Table 2 continued

	Fall 2005			Spring 2006		
	N	% of agree	mean	*N*	% of agree	mean
Out-of-Class Activity Western's FYE program encourages students to become involved in campus activities.	97	89.7	4.6	72	90.4	4.7
Out-of-Class Activity Western's FYE program helps students appreciate that learning extends beyond the classroom.	97	84.5	4.3	70	82.2	4.4
I attend out-of-class activities with this FYE class.	96	85.6	5.0	73	87.7	5.0

Findings

The design elements that addressed interpersonal relations and exposure to out-of- class experiences generally were rated quite favorably. Responses by both students and faculty indicate that the majority of students felt valued by their FYE instructors, and first-year students felt comfortable in talking with faculty, especially about academic difficulties. Responses suggest that first-year students were not quite as comfortable talking with peer mentors. Both students and faculty overwhelmingly indicated that class discussion was promoted.

First-year students indicated that they were definitely aware of out-of-class activities and that they believed that attending these events was included in their FYE course grades. They were somewhat less likely to say they attended and appreciated those activities. FYE faculty were more positive that the FYE program encouraged students to become involved in activities, and the faculty were likely to have attended those activities with their students.

Conclusion

As evidenced above, our FYE program has had an acute and positive effect on student-faculty interaction. An important question now is how does FYE class interaction affect long-term academic success? Likewise, the evidence suggests an increased awareness of campus community activities and modest gains in participation. Will this affect student engagement in their remaining years at WIU?

Based on our experiences, institutions that are considering using this approach to offering an academic component of a FYE program should

- Ensure that there is both top-level administrative support for FYE classes and faculty buy-in for this class-based model
- Create job responsibilities in FYE course management for mid-level management
- Choose classes to be offered with the FYE designation that are already valued by faculty (e.g., general education courses)
- Invest financial support to offer replacement coursework for students displaced by small FYE enrollments (if necessary)

There is very strong campus support for the FYE courses component of our FYE program, particularly from the university president. The university is currently committed to continuing to offer FYE courses to all incoming first-year students and is beginning to work toward institutionalizing the program.

Primary Contributor

Judith M. Dallinger
Assistant Provost for Undergraduate Studies
Provost's Office
Western Illinois University
Macomb, IL 61455
Phone: 309-298-1066
E-mail: J-Dallinger@wiu.edu

Additional Contributor

Matthew Blankenship
Professor
Western Illinois University

About the Editors

Marc Cutright is associate professor of Higher Education and director of the Center for Higher Education at the University of North Texas. At North Texas, he is involved with the Institute for the Study of Transfer Students and is the university's first Professor in Residence, living in a residence hall as a general resource to students. He is a co-author of *Achieving and Sustaining Institutional Excellence for the First Year of College* (Jossey-Bass, 2005) and was a research associate with the Policy Center on the First Year of College. His Ed.D. is from the University of Tennessee at Knoxville. During those studies, he was a Fulbright Scholar to Canada.

Wendy G. Troxel is an assistant professor in the Department of Educational Administration and Foundations at Illinois State University, teaching graduate-level research methods courses in quantitative and qualitative designs, program evaluation and assessment, and The American College Student. Previously, she served the campus as director of the University Assessment Office, coordinating student learning outcomes research and assisting faculty and staff with the development, implementation, and use of assessment activities to improve learning and development. She earned her doctorate in educational leadership at the University of Alabama at Birmingham, with emphases in educational research and education law.

Index

Alphabetical Listing of Institutions

Four-Year Institutions